MONE

 a beginner's guide

CHRISTEEN SKINNER

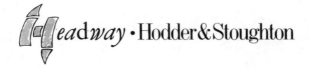

MONEY SIGNS
a beginner's guide

Order queries: please contact Bookpoint Ltd, 39 Milton Park, Abingdon, Oxon OX14
4TD. Telephone: (44) 01235 400414, Fax: (44) 01235 400454. Lines are open from
9.00–6.00, Monday to Saturday, with a 24 hour message answering service. Email
address: orders@bookpoint.co.uk

A catalogue record for this title is available from The British Library

ISBN 0 340 72083 2

First published 1998
Impression number 10 9 8 7 6 5 4 3 2 1
Year   2003 2002 2001 2000 1999 1998

Typeset by Transet Limited, Coventry, England.
Printed in Great Britain for Hodder & Stoughton Educational, a division of Hodder
Headline plc, 338 Euston Road, London NW1 3BH by Cox and Wyman Limited,
Reading, Berks.

CONTENTS

Dedication

The challenge of writing a first book is daunting and I am grateful to the very many people who believed that I could do it. Teresa Moorey in particular deserves much thanks for instigating the introduction to Hodder Headline.

When I was ten, my much loved Aunt Dorothy bought me a book called *Being a Writer*. I would like to thank her for the confidence she had in me then and apologise too, for the fact that it took nearly 40 years to fulfil that early promise.

In January 1998, when this book was taking up large parts of every day, my husband, Michael, gave all the support I needed to enable me to meet the deadline. My daughter Claire, gave constructive criticism reading each section as it was written and returning it the following morning with helpful comment. I am indebted to them both for their love and encouragement. Finally, I wish my parents had been alive to see the start of this new career.

INTRODUCTION

In this book we are going to look at the way in which each Sun sign of the zodiac reacts to financial and business affairs. Before doing so, however, we should take note of the great importance of the Sun in all our daily lives. We readily acknowledge that the planets journey around the Sun but we are, perhaps, not as aware that as the planets orbit our Sun, their combined gravitational pull creates disturbances in the Sun's behaviour. The existence of sunspots and solar flares has been known for thousands of years. However, we now know that the Sun also spins on its axis and that this spin can be affected when the large 'gassy' planets (Jupiter, Saturn, Uranus and Neptune) take up a particular alignment. Although this has happened only seven times in the last 3,500 years, we know that the Earth is changed dramatically by the unusual, subsequent, weather patterns. Two instances stand out. The weather which followed the configuration of 1632 saw fairs held on the frozen ice of the River Thames in London. There were short growing seasons and 1641 saw the worst winter of the century for the Americas. The next instance of the Sun retrograde was in 1810; 1816 was the year without a summer when North Eastern USA and Western Europe had freezing weather every month of the year. This, in turn, gave way to a succession of short summers and long, cold winters triggering famine in Switzerland and the Ukraine.

In April 1989, the Sun's spin was affected as described above and we should anticipate that weather patterns from that time will be severely distorted. It is hard to say how long this will last, but past indicators would suggest that in excess of a decade may be likely. When world weather differs from what is expected, crop growing

suffers seriously. There are two major results to be expected from this. First, commodity prices rise (i.e. Corn Flakes, etc. will cost more) and second, populations may be displaced by those who are hungry moving to areas of the world where they feel more sure of being fed. Both of these scenarios affect the economy of the world in general. Many people acknowledge that the weather has been significantly inconstant in recent years and that the lives of many have been seriously inconvenienced by natural disasters which may be seen to be weather related.

It will be of great assistance to many to have understanding of other planet cycles operating in the coming years. This, combined with acknowledgement of each Sun sign's particular ways of dealing with financial matters, should be of benefit to those living during these times.

We are going to look at some of the major planet cycles and how these affect economics generally. We will follow the generational effect of the two planets Jupiter and Saturn as they affect ways of financial thinking and go on to look at how each Sun sign of the zodiac handles money and matters related to it.

It is, of course, absolutely essential to remember that the position of the Sun at birth is only part of the horoscope story. Your horoscope – literally 'map of the hour', gives details of the positions of the planets as seen from Earth at a given time and place. These 'maps of the hours' should; in fact, be 'maps of minutes' as it has to be remembered that cycles are ever changing so that every minute makes a real difference.

In Chapter 4 of this book, the financial traits of each of the twelve Sun sign positions are portrayed. If you were born between the 19th and 23rd of any month, you will have to consider yourself as being 'cuspal', that is, unless you have had a full chart mapped for you, you will have to read the portrait of the next-door sign which might be more fitting for you. Remember, there are 365 or 366 days in the year. The Sun moves through 360 degrees. The difference means that the moment at which the Sun changes signs is variable. At the end of this book you will find a list of helpful addresses if you require further information.

An astrologer takes account not only of the position of the Sun, but also of the Moon and planets at birth. It is only through study of the whole chart that really helpful judgements can be made. It is hoped that this book will prove to be an introduction for many who are interested in the part that the planets play in world economics and in their own personal financial dealings.

In the final chapter of the book you will find some ideas as to how the various Sun signs may experience the challenges of the planet movements in the first decade of the twenty-first century. This is no substitute for a full analysis of a personal chart but should throw helpful pointers as to the coming period.

WHAT IS TRADE?

We should all be aware that in days of old, humans bartered for everything that they were unable to provide for themselves. A pig might be traded for a certain amount of wheat, or milk for honey. It was some considerable time before currency was in regular use. The concept of currency goes back to antiquity and through the study of ancient coins it has been possible to unearth the secrets of the everyday life of a variety of cultures. The figureheads on those coins are fascinating. We know that it is these people and their wealth which enabled entrepreneurs to have the essential capital to undertake huge journeys through which it was hoped that trade would begin. In these early times, it would have been almost impossible for someone not born into nobility to gain wealth – unless, of course, they had a skill which they could sell. Those without adequate capital of their own were in no position to become involved in projects which might yield good financial return.

Midway through the fifteenth century the first company was formed. The word company – derived from *com pagnie* (Italian for 'with bread') describes those deals done in the coffee houses of Amsterdam and London when the cost of shipping enterprises was shared between a number of dealers, each of whom took 'shares' in the project. The Cabot company – the first known company – was formed in 1528, and required that merchants each purchase a twenty-five pound investment in a specific shipping enterprise. Each of these merchants took a major risk and hoped that their capital would be realised at the end of the trip and that an amount of interest would have been earned. The investment represented a major part of the merchant's capital, but it was still only a proportion

of the money needed for these enterprises to set forth. These then, were the first 'shares'. Since that time, share ownership has been open to many. In the twentieth century, 'Penny Shares' gained popularity and a greater proportion of the populace became share holders than ever before. Even those who did not own actual shares themselves, often had their pension policies linked to the market place.

The extent to which people are involved in financial and business affairs has grown and the time has come when an understanding of how these attitudes correlate with a person's Sun sign position is helpful. First, however, in order to see why these issues are becoming more important, we need to look at how the broad sweep of large planetary cycles has affected humankind.

What is interesting from an astrological point of view is that the first company came into being after the first Neptune Pluto conjunction to occur in the sign of Gemini for over 3,000 years. Gemini is the sign connected with trade and communication. Standing on Earth, it appears that Neptune and Pluto are aligned in a straight line approximately every 496 years. This is known as their geocentric conjunction. Each successive conjunction is approximately 7 degrees further on in the zodiac from the last. So it was that the first Gemini – trading – conjunction occurred in 1398. The next was in 1891, there will be another in 2400 and so on. It will not be until nearly the year 4000 AD, that the conjunctions will move away from the commercial sign of Gemini and into Cancer.

The Neptune Pluto cycle is yielding information as to possible links between it and times of commercial boom and bust. Neptune is, after all, the planet associated with fraud and with inflation, whilst Pluto is the great God of Wealth and revitalisation. Working together they can combine to distort matters on a grand scale or bring out creative talent that seems 'out of this world'.

This book is concerned with the period between 1998 and 2008 and how business and financial matters are likely to develop. The most recent Neptune Pluto cycle began in 1891 and is still in its infancy. However, we have seen already that distortion of trade through prohibition, drug money and money laundering has taken place on

a large scale since that time. Neptune rules alcohol, pharmaceutical products and anything to do with water whilst Pluto rules great wealth and large volume trading. During this same period we have also seen the birth of creative accountancy and novel ways of trading being underwritten by consortiums of banks. The world of finance is certainly changing but in the process is anything but secure. Drug money and money laundering alone distort calculations and the problem is now so insidious on the world banking stage that accountability is a long way off. Currency crises have been many and, without the International Monetary Fund, many countries would now be bankrupt. Even the intervention of the IMF and World Bank has not been sufficient to prevent difficulties for some nations and, around the world, many are becoming aware that the global network, far from strengthening positions, may be leaving more people financially or materially vulnerable.

It is unlikely that these problems will diminish in the coming years. Since Pluto's move into Sagittarius in 1997, we are likely to see ever grander international financial scandals hit the headlines. In January 1998, Neptune made its move into Aquarius for the first time since 1831. Neptune, the planet associated as much with idealism as it is with fraud, does not work especially well in the Air sign of Aquarius. This time round, we may hear of grandiose idealistic financial schemes which are supposed to be universally beneficial but which require constant vigilance if unscrupulous people are not to defraud people both on an individual and national level. Aquarius is the most futuristic of all signs so that the Options markets are thrown into sharp focus when any planet passes through this sign. With Neptune passing through this sign we may find that fraud and manipulation of the Option and Derivate markets create chaos. We should note too, that as Neptune's effect seems to inflate everything, markets followed their astrological forecast and soared to dizzying heights on the very day that Neptune went into Aquarius in January 1998. Astrologically we should forewarn that this is unlikely to be sustained and that Saturn will prick this bubble later in the year.

The good news is that Uranus is presently moving through its own sign of Aquarius and will continue this passage until 2004. Uranus, the truth seeker and harbinger of an enlightenment, should give each of us a shake as it makes this passage. It should make us all aware of our very individual responses to financial affairs and the need for honesty and integrity to be applied. Inevitably, new regulations will have to be applied. These may be stringent but should prevent the more honest from being deceived by the unscrupulous.

In short, the coming years will see massive changes in the way in which financial matters are regulated. Indeed, we may see that money itself is radically altered. New currencies will appear. In some parts, cash itself may be replaced by smart card systems. Every individual will be affected by the changes and their reactions will be different; based first on the generation from which they come and second on their Sun sign.

2 GENERATIONAL INFLUENCES

So far we have seen that the evolution of business and financial affairs is long and encompasses some of the cycles of the outer planets particularly. Before looking at how each sign of the zodiac reacts to the subject, we need to look at one other planet cycle. This one could almost be described as a generational cycle. Few would disagree that different generations have dealt with monetary affairs in quite different ways. Each has its own way of looking at things and both banks and governments have changed their rules and regulations at intervals so that each successive generation has to respond to these variations as well as to their own particular point of view.

Jupiter and Saturn play out different roles for us. Jupiter, the largest of the planets that we know of, is seen as expansive, optimistic, courageous, bold, dramatic and expensive. Saturn assumes the role of cosmic banker and appears pessimistic, cautious, prudent and thrifty. Each and every one of us us has these two planets in our charts and the struggle between them can be a determining factor in assessing our entrepreneurship. If we are too Saturnian – or cautious – we may miss a good opportunity. On the other hand, if we are Jupiterian, we may stand accused of being foolhardy, cavalier and prone to taking too many risks. Of course, there may be times when the risk pays off but it is equally probable that there will be times when an enterprise is sunk through lack of care and attention.

Having these two planets in balance to one another is the ideal. If we are born at a time when they are conjunct (together), we understand both influences and blend them well. Born when they are at half (opposition) or quarter (square) way points in their 360-

degree journey, the fight between the two is so strong that we react by going from one extreme to another. At one time we may be confident that we are taking an educated gamble and at other times determine that we can afford no risk whatsoever. By taking up these polar opposite positions, our business affairs may suffer through our inconsistent strategy.

When the two planets are at either sextile or trine (60 or 120 degrees from one another) it is possible that we may have the balance just right. Our instincts, if all else is well in the chart, may show us to be able to balance these two divergent attitudes and so contain sustained growth of our financial affairs. What we notice on a global scale is that, when the two planets are conjunct, we enter into a new economic phase which is adjusted at the time of the square and comes to a critical point at the time of the opposition.

The pattern of the these two planetary orbits is that they are conjunct every twenty years. The dance is a little more complicated in that after several conjunctions in one element (Fire, Earth, Air or Water) the conjunction moves on to take place in the next element. The twentieth century conjunctions have taken place as follows: 1901 in Capricorn, 1921 in Virgo, 1940 in Taurus, 1961 in Capricorn – all Earth sign conjunctions. There will be a further Earth conjunction in May 2000 in Taurus. What is interesting is that, unusually, the conjunction in 1981 was in the Air sign of Libra. The conjunctions which take place after May 2000 will move on into the Air series. The 1981 conjunction was, therefore, most unusual.

As the 1961 pattern began to decline after the two planets were exactly 180 degrees (opposition) from one another in 1970, the pull into the Air sign conjunction began to take effect. What was noticeable in this period was that hire purchase and other credit schemes gained ground. It seemed that everyone was able to borrow on the 'never-never'. No longer was it necessary to save up before purchasing. It was possible for many people to have a product when they wanted it and on the supposition that they would have the wherewithal to pay for it over a period of time. An escalation in the price of some products was probably inevitable as the focus was on the monthly repayments as opposed to the total price due. This was

a period for ideas; grand in scale and small in practicality. Older generations, who had the very earthy concept of saving first and spending later, found the new attitude difficult. It was hard for them to be supportive of their young whom they saw to be burdening themselves with ever greater debt.

The 'yuppie' era of the 1980s coincided with a time of boom. It seemed that everything was on the upward march. From housing to indexes, growth seemed assured. However, the cycle has its peaks and troughs and as the planets Jupiter and Saturn came to critical points, what was overvalued was sure to be re-evaluated. The stock market crashes of 1987 and 1989 witnessed loss on a massive scale and, eventually, led to a new kind of thinking being adopted. It was, by now, clear that the rise could not continue and that some general levelling would take place. Banking crises fell hard on the heels of these developments and many discovered the shocking fact that what had appeared to be safe was not.

Towards the end of the twentieth century, and in acknowledgment of the new Jupiter Saturn cycle due to start in May 2000, the accent is turning once more toward the idea of security in the form of capital. No longer will it be acceptable to borrow against future earnings. The concept of saving first and spending later is coming back into vogue.

Clearly there are some Sun signs which will respond to this initiative more than others. Equally, however, there are some generations who will find it easier to return to an old philosophy. Those born between the endings of the two world wars have lived through similar cycles before and are well equipped to show how thrift and saving can work. The task will be much harder for those born since the Second World War who have lived through the long 'credit' years and who will now have to be re-educated. Perhaps it will be hardest of all for those born since the last Earth cycle began in 1960. These young people have never known any other financial system other than that which has been based on credit rating. The coming years may be hard for them as they discover that no matter how good the rating, the cash is not available.

Older generations will find the return to old ways comforting and, free of the burden of debt, discover a happiness long forgotten.

ARIES

A ries is a Fire sign. These people are productive and excel when they have a project, a *raison d'être*, an aim or a mission. Aries people do not need someone to think up an idea for them; being creative individuals, they are quite capable of coming up with something themselves. Their attitude is ever changing. Fire is never constant and can go from dying ember to furnace in a relatively short time. So it is with Aries' general attitude to finance – they may experience the whole gamut from having no financial resources to having plenty. Because this happens quite regularly, they develop a generally *laissez-faire* attitude to money in the wallet or purse. Cash appears to flow through at speed but is not something that Aries people are going to worry about too much. The ups and downs

happen so regularly that they know that an up turn in their fortunes can happen as quickly as a down turn. What would worry them is a feeling of stagnation. If there is no movement whatsoever, Aries is apt to create it and, when this happens, the result can all too often be negative.

This is not to say that Aries people are unable to treasure the cash they hold. It is simply that knowledge of what their cash looks and feels like is not a major factor for them. They may not even know how much cash they are carrying. To know such things goes against another Aries characteristic – that of impulsive and instinctive behaviour. Getting in touch with such mundane matters as cash, they feel, might attract a careworn-ness or worry factor which they do not need to have as part of their make-up.

Nor is it likely to be part of their habit pattern to fold bills neatly or to keep coins of different denominations in different pockets. It is not that they are incapable of doing this. In fact, once the suggestion is made that, by keeping their purse tidy, they may attract more resources, they will give it a try. The effort is likely to be short lived, however, since this group lose patience if something does not appear to work immediately.

The speed of credit/debit card transactions appeals to this group and offers a means by which they can take control of their financial situation. Aries people are less likely to spend funds on frivolous items once they have learnt that their main account is affected immediately. Of course, this is something that they only learn by experience but the important thing is that they do learn – although the process may take some time!

All told, cash is an irritant to Aries people. It can all too easily become a chore to look after. Foreign currency can be twice as irritating – especially when very small coins are involved. This group of people, for whom time is of the essence, do not want to be burdened either with bulky coins, or the need to fiddle about counting out their cash. Paying by paper currency is always going to take precedence over making up a sum by coins – for them, that is a task best suited to those who have more time on their hands!

When it comes to bartering or negotiating a price for something, Aries people have no problem in speaking up for what they want. In fact, they can be hagglers *extra ordinaire* and wear the other person down with their determination to get what they want at the price they are prepared to pay for it. Negotiating brings out their competitive spirit and one can be assured that they will stay with the fight until they have won.

Saving is often a problem area for Aries people. Essentially they see this as a passive and, therefore, boring exercise. For them, the need to see funds grow quickly is paramount. They are exasperated by those schemes which require a certain level of investment just to get started. Aries people need to feel that they can contribute a little or a lot as and when they want to. Freedom here is very important. The idea of having their money safely 'locked up' for long periods of time may appeal intellectually, but the reality of not having the option of being able to take the money out on demand to snap up some offer or other, rules out long-term saving commitments.

Aries people value freedom and being independent. That said, they are usually involved in a partnership somewhere in their lives. One could argue that they need the partnership just to show how 'free' and independent of spirit they really are. So it is with financial partnerships. They like the idea and may feel that the other party will provide security and underpinning for their own quirks. However, they react badly if they find their spending controlled by another. Trust and honesty are vital issues here. They have respect for other people's caution but require that others respect their need to be free to do their own thing.

A common feature of those born under a Fire sign is a willingness to take risk and to seize upon a moment of opportunity. In this, they have been known to take inspired gambles. Aries people can back a hunch and identify a product that is going to have incredible public appeal. They are not the only sign of the zodiac able to do this, but they are, perhaps, one of the few signs that will go out of their way to back a project in its early stages. This does not, of course, mean that all their 'hunches' will prove to be right and part of the learning process for the young Aries investor is in learning that it is as well to

13

do some elementary checking of information before rushing in. This is where a partnership can really help. If Aries investors can pass on the idea of a scoop to someone else to do the checking for them, then so much the better.

The concept of investment planning may be perceived as long range commitment and will then be anathema to Aries people. Were one trying to 'sell' the idea of investment planning to an Aries, it might be better explained as strategic saving. This kind of language infers some sort of military planning with an ever-readiness to seize the main chance and score a win over others. The Aries portfolio will include young stocks. The stocks are usually sufficiently aged to be starting to show promise but a long way from fulfilment. Here, Aries people would seem to have the knack for seeing the potential and for buying in at the optimum moment before the stock price takes off. With older stocks, it seems that Aries people have the happy knack of being able to buy in just as they are reaching a market bottom and selling out near a market top.

It should always be remembered that Aries people are ruled by the fast-action planet Mars. Aries people need to be able to take action quickly – at a moment's notice if need be. Much as a cat about to pounce, the Aries person enjoys the feeling that they were the ones ready in place at the right time and willing to make a move. But it is the move and the thrill that is critical here. Holding stocks for years and years waiting for them to rise is simply not for an Aries. They need the option of being able to move on quickly and to be free to re-invest in something more dynamic.

Those born under the sign of Aries are classically good self investors or entrepreneurs. They have no problem with backing one of their own ideas and are energised by resistance from bankers. Proving that they can make something work and that they are leaders in the field is a great feeling for them. Investing in themselves is no problem at all. Their weakness lies in that they function poorly when asked to do repetitive jobs over long periods of time and that they tend to be poor delegators. Their enthusiasm can wane all too easily and with all the knowledge of the business being carried by them alone, they rarely have backup support people ready to take over when they lose energy. Where they have great talent, however,

is in having one eye forever on the future. Their fear of stagnation is such that they are permanently attuned to ideas that will keep their business and its products in the lead. This is true even for those in service industries. By revamping the service regularly – and this too is a form of self-investment, they ensure that their service maintains its appeal and that their financial futures are secure.

PRACTICE

1 At the end of each day empty your purse or pocket of change. Start to save one kind of coin in a jar on the top left- hand side of a bedroom table.
2 Make sure that your purse or wallet can look after your money. It should be strong and quite big.
3 Use your debit card more than your credit card.
4 Check your bank statement monthly.
5 Buy yourself a premium or savings bond every birthday.
6 When saving for something specific, always have a picture of the object in a prominent position.

Taurus

15

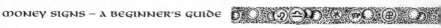

Taureans are the great appreciators of the zodiac. From the most simple to the most elaborate; from no expense to vast expense; Taurus gains pleasure. However, Taureans are aware that they are going to have to develop some financial acumen if they are going to be able to live their life of 'Wine and Song'. To provide for both themselves and others in the way that they wish requires that they gain an understanding of money and finance, and so they set themselves on this road fairly early on – discovering that 'taking care of the pennies' results in 'pounds taking care of themselves'. Coins and paper currency are treated well by Taureans and kept tidily to prevent any muddle. Taureans take care of their cash and will try not to split paper currency until absolutely necessary. They would rather take time to see if they can make up the required sum from loose change or small denomination notes or bills. Taureans develop a careful and controlled approach to cash and arrive at a routine for emptying pockets and checking change carefully.

They are not impulse spenders and, in fact, can find the whole shopping process tedious. They have to be in the mood but once they are, they are drawn to those items which offer durability as much as quality. It is quite likely that they will have taken time to do some window shopping – if only subconsciously – before making their final commitment to purchase. It is also probable that they will have saved up the right amount and will prefer to pay cash rather than run up a credit charge.

In their choice of bank, Taureans gravitate toward a bank that presents conservative appeal. They do not want to have to grapple with new ideas from the banking community but want a straightforward service. Home banking may sound like a nice idea to them, but the reality of having to master any new technology would curtail such an exercise very quickly. The new smart card payment systems which do away with cash entirely are unlikely to appeal to this group who favour more traditional methods. It has even taken them some time to come to terms with debit and cash cards. Taureans juggle these with ease and make use of them in a practical way. It is unlikely they will run up huge debts with credit cards and they are likely to make a note in their diaries as to payment date

and make sure that they clear their account as swiftly as possible. It is often said that Taureans are the natural bankers of the zodiac. Ruled by Venus, they have a wonderful understanding of the need to balance income and expenditure. They know the importance of building a sound capital base and good credit rating.

When travelling abroad leads them to having to deal with different currencies, Taureans appreciate those coinages which have a solid feel to them. Those coins which are made up of different alloys, and which carry no 'weight' to them, will tend to be regarded with disdain. Similarly, paper currency which has a frivolous look to it and is in high denomination will also be regarded as inferior. Taureans do not want to have to pay in thousand units for a simple loaf of bread and will fail to understand why the numbers cannot be rationalised. It is at times like these that the Taurus starts to appreciate credit cards where payments will eventually be made in their own currency which they know and trust.

The accent for Taureans is always on security, but that does not mean that those of this sign are unable to enjoy the moment. This group loves to enjoy a good night out, whether this be at the local pub or in a fine restaurant. They also see artistic pleasures as being as valuable as food itself. Security for Taureans means ensuring that the larder contains all the basic products and that there are also some luxury items to complement these. They have clear focus as to the standard of living that they wish to attain and move with steady determination toward that goal.

For Taureans, savings are most commonly linked to real estate purchase. This forms their future security. Taureans see the most natural investment as being in bricks and mortar. Even here, their need to know exactly where they stand will show in their choice of mortgage repayment scheme. Not being risk takers, they gravitate toward a simple repayment scheme and it would take a good salesman to convince them of the value of a pension linked mortgage or index-linked endowment. The possibility that the value of the fund might not be sufficient to pay off the mortgage at the appropriate time turns them off the idea altogether. Drawn only toward those advertisements which emphasise security and

simplicity, they turn away from new deals on the high street that may have a better return but look too complicated or have an element of risk attached.

Choosing Taureans as financial partners usually proves to be a wise choice. Those of this sign understand that joy and fun are an integral part of life and balance this with the needs of practical living. Your money will be safe in Taurus' hands and there is the added benefit of a partner who understands the need to indulge in a little frivolous spending from time to time. It is not easy to persuade Taureans to change their opinions. They are courteous in argument but show no inclination to adopt a different stance to one already taken. Taurus' stubbornness and obstinacy is legendary. It would be almost impossible to convince Taureans that you had a 'safe bet' in mind. If betting is involved, they do not want to know. Taureans are better in situations where they are able to do things in their own way and in their own time.

When it comes to negotiating, Taureans don't. They determine what they are prepared to pay for a product or service and wait for the other party to realise that it is the only price they are going to pay. The debate may start genially enough but it will not be long before it is apparent that Taurus has no intention whatsoever of moving from their original position. Their persistence and determination is renowned. They may be calm and charming but they are not going to change tack. If provoked, negotiations will break down completely. An angry or outraged Taurus really can be like the bull in the china shop and break everything in sight rendering any further dialogue useless.

Should they be attracted to equities or inherit shares, Taureans take the view that building society or bank schemes which have a proven record will suit them best. It would take quite some salesman to convince those of this sign that some new fund investing in young companies overseas would offer the best gain. When pressed to pick stocks on their own, they tend to go for blue chip companies whose value over time seems to move steadily upwards. Food products, commodities and the entertainment industry all have appeal for Taurus. However, they need the services of a broker to manage these

stocks for them. Taureans are generally just too slow in their pace to carve their way through the frenzy of the stock exchange floor. The whirlwind of prices going through limits that the Taurus has fixed in his mind makes this an alien place. Treasury Bonds appeal to Taureans. These are subject to markedly less volatility and, although returns are not guaranteed, a moderate rate of growth usually applies.

Taureans may be great appreciators and have a taste for the finer things in life, but their personal creativity does not work well in the area of entrepreneurship. Taureans may be artistic but this does not extend to having grand visionary ideas to bring to fruition. Taureans are superb generals. They can follow other peoples' commands to the letter. They also know exactly how to bring production costs down to a minimum. However, they are not natural salespeople, and neither do they have good marketing skills. Since they are not quick on the uptake, it is all too easy for a deal to pass them by. Running their own business then, is fraught with difficulties and it is all too easy for them to be overtaken by others. However, as with the tortoise and the hare, they always get to where they wanted to be at the end of the day. They may choose to avoid the stress and strain of owning their own business and choose instead to be managing directors for someone else. In this position, they command good earnings and enjoy a material level of comfort that is the envy of many.

PRACTICE

1 Read about one technical advance each week. Make a note of the companies involved and watch for their share listing.
2 Buy yourself some shares for your birthday each year. These shares should be linked to new advances.
3 Make an appointment with your bank manager. Have new style accounts explained in person.
4 Before using foreign currency, spend one evening getting familiar with it.
5 Find a way of investing in the arts.
6 Read at least one book about an entrepreneur each year.

Gemini

Geminis develop a flexible attitude to money and, as with most things in their life, money proves an area open to lively debate and full of conversational opportunities. There is little that Gemini people like better than to have something to talk about; views on finance, dialogue about financial exchange and proposals about investment planning prove stimulating to those of this sign. It is not at all uncommon to hear of Geminis bartering in their financial negotiations even when they live in Western areas of the world where haggling over price is not necessarily experienced on a daily basis. Bartering is a form of conversation and is also a source of information. In debating the value of goods, Gemini people will hope to learn more about the goods themselves. There is plenty of opportunity to ask yet another question under these conditions and, of course, anything that prolongs conversation appeals to Gemini.

A pocket full of cash can give great pleasure to Gemini people since it can be an agent to getting what they desire most – information. Cash to them falls into two separate types: coinage and paper currency. Their attitude to coinage can be almost careless and they may show scant regard for checking their change. The same is not true of their attitude to paper currency which they treasure infinitely more carefully, since it affords a very different kind of opportunity. Geminis have a natural sense of fun based primarily on extracting information from one source to pass on to another. The time taken to

extricate a bill or note from their purse or wallet also gives time to add another comment to any discussion. Notes may be folded in all sorts of ways and kept in many pockets, but Gemini people know exactly where each one is kept even if they give the appearance of being distracted trying to remember exactly where the banknote they are looking for is. The more colourful the banknote, the more they appreciate it. Foreign currency is not a problem for them and has great appeal since they enjoy the mental calisthenics of calculating back and forth and checking daily exchange rates. Charge cards may allow for greater flexibility in spending but Gemini people are unlikely to gain as much pleasure from using these as they do from using cash. It is true that they use charge card flexibility to 'rob Peter to pay Paul' when they have more than one credit card, but they can also get themselves into something of a financial mess by running up bills which become ever harder to pay off. Remembering exactly what they owe to which charge card is difficult and it will not be long before they discover that they have come to the limit on each card.

Budgeting is not an easy task for Gemini. It may be intellectually satisfying to work out a budget, but putting this into practice is anything but simple. Geminis can always think of a way of bending the rules – even if these are rules that they have set themselves. Having bent the rules, it is not long before the complexity of these 'deals within deals' leads them into difficulties. There is, however, perhaps no other sign better able to talk their way out of trouble. They are always able to find a way of consolidating their debt at a better rate of interest. Once they have set up a pattern for paying off debt, and paid it off, it is not long before they see that they could continue to set aside the same sum for a savings scheme.

Geminis are attracted to savings schemes and enjoy the considerable sport to be had in the banter of comparing one savings scheme with another. Unlike many other signs, it is common for Gemini to become interested in several different schemes – partly to spread their capital base, but also as a means of always having something to compare. This allows Geminis that essential versatility which is crucial to their well being. The idea of building up savings levels appeals to this group. As they move from one level to another and receive higher levels of interest as a result, they become ever more

interested in how the rates are calculated. Questions may need to be asked and the ensuing discussion finds them arriving at a better deal as a result. Moving their savings from one scheme to another in pursuit of greater profit can become something of a habit for those of this sign. To avoid this, and the potential losses that can be incurred through defaulting on commitment, they need savings schemes which are updated annually and take into account any budget or tax incentives. In this way, they gain confidence in an account which is managed to accommodate changing conditions and feel less need to make changes themselves.

It is not at all unusual to find that Gemini people are involved in at least one financial partnership. In this however, they may prove to be quite unstable. It is in the Gemini nature to resist any course of action which they may perceive as tying them down for too long a period of time. It is essential for any partner to understand this and to take steps to comply with the flexibility that Gemini requires. A partner who insisted on fixed 'five year planning' would find themselves dealing with considerable resistence from a Gemini partner. Gemini might enjoy the initial discussions and planning, but keeping to it would be very difficult indeed. An irritant for those in financial partnership with Geminis is their inability to keep receipts for cash expenses in one safe place. The tendency to stuff the receipt inside their bag, where it becomes lost in chaos, can be quite tiresome. It is not that they are incapable of being methodical, it is just that their brain is always dealing with several matters at one time and it is unlikely that receipt management has high priority! To be financially successful in a project requires that Gemini's considerable mental energy is in constant use. It is when they are bored that those of this sign sabotage their own objectives. Distracted by something which seems more rewarding for the moment, they fail to give due concentration to the business plan in hand. It is essential, therefore, that for financial success, there is a partner in the wings who is happy to maintain constant monitoring of the project. It is also valuable if that person has the ability to coax them back to thinking about the original task and to re-enthuse Gemini for the project.

The concept of share dealing is appealing to Geminis. Well-spread risk is an exciting concept to them. Nor will they shrink from investing in new and small companies. In fact, their very inquisitiveness may lead them to gathering information in areas that even the most seasoned financial journalist has not yet sought out. A varied portfolio then is comforting to those of this sign who, if so inclined, will spend much time getting hold of the various balance sheets necessary to make their financial judgements. Since they want to dip in and out of the market quickly, their relationship with their stockbroker is vital. Geminis want easy transactions and minimal paperwork but they also need someone available with whom they can bounce off ideas and strategies and who will comply with their requests promptly.

In their spending habits, Geminis have a tendency to break their pre-set budget regularly. It may be that they underestimate expenses. If it is not in pushing their travel allowance over the limit, it is in the purchase of magazines and books. It would be interesting to know just how many of these are actually read! Telephone bills are also likely to exceed any agreed limit. Not to have contacts or information is most upsetting for Gemini people but it is possible that they could be more prudent with these expenses. Geminis make some of the best technical analysts of the zodiac but even here they are not afraid of spending money on information from which to glean ever more information. They may be information junkies and be paying needlessly high prices. It is quite possible that poring over analysis results in them missing optimum moments in the markets. They can be distracted from the main objective all too easily – whether it be by a chart, a discussion or a phone call and thus miss the vital moment.

Geminis have to foster concentration so that fine ideas can be turned into practical moves. Entrepreneurial zeal is encouraged through contacts. Talk fosters ideas which in turn foster more ideas. It is relatively simple for Gemini people to talk others into investing capital in a new project that they have just come up with. The problem is that Gemini can all too easily overlook the fact that this capital is vitally important to the other person. Where Gemini people may not be too concerned if things do not work out well, the

other party just might be. Geminis have a gift for being able to pick themselves up and starting all over again. Others may not have the same skill and be badly hurt by a Gemini investment.

PRACTICE

1 Play at being thrifty one day in every week.
2 Have only one credit card.
3 Have a piggy bank by the phone. Put something in for every outgoing call.
4 Get a group of friends together and pool resources for a share portfolio. Meet monthly to monitor your investment.
5 Subscribe to only one investment magazine. Get other advice from a quality newspaper.
6 Give yourself money for your birthday. Put this into an account that you won't touch for at least five years.

Cancer

Security is a major issue for those born under this sign and it follows that their attitude to money is serious as a result. It would be unthinkable for Cancerians to run short of money and, on the few occasions in their life when they do, the effect on their emotional well-being is dramatic. Whatever age they are, once they recognise

this money–mood link, they start to take interest in financial dealings. In youth this may be by way of watching how others handle their financial affairs. Once they have charge of their own finances they can exhibit a maturity that is surprising.

Cancerians generally do not feel the need to have purses or wallets containing a wad of notes or bills. They may own a variety of purses and wallets and ensure that each is left with a little something in them 'just in case'. Cancerians have wonderful memories and can remember how certain coins came to be in their purse – a find, a saving, a gift. In this way, cash is treasured as with everything else that they own. They are not mean, but will be reluctant to part with these treasured possessions since it may feel as though they are parting with a memory at the same time. If they do part with it, it must be for a very good reason. Some would describe them as hoarders and it is certainly true that they have a reluctance to throw anything away. However, it is a Cancerian talent to see that everything has its time and some things have their time more than once! On the basis that there is still some value to be had, they store many things for another occasion. In this way they ensure that there is always provision for emergencies and, as a result, the Cancerian capital base grows and grows.

It is important for money to be kept safely and Cancerians may feel that their purse or wallet is insufficiently secure for larger sums of cash. This means choosing a bank. Trust is an issue for Cancerians and learning to deal with banks and other investment houses is a difficult concept – at least in the early years. Cancerians expect that their money will be looked after and this means 'their' money; so that in one sense, they want to be given back exactly the same note that they deposited there in the first place. It takes time for Cancerians to accept that this will not be the case and that the bank will take 'their' money, invest it and give back another note plus interest. The relationship with bank cashiers and managers is important here too. Continuity, stability, confidentiality and reliability are all key concerns and it is unsettling when Cancerians have to forge new relationships with those who look after their financial affairs.

Cancerians are canny shoppers and ensure that each purchase gives value for money. With the exception of basic commodities, they buy with the intention of using goods for some considerable time and so look for a certain quality along with good value. They take some pride in recycling goods. Aside from family heirlooms, which they would cherish anyway, Cancerians love to get hold of an item that has clearly been well loved and cared for. They buy quality goods second hand and revitalise these by giving them their own special touch. With basic commodities, food stuffs, etc. the Cancerian eye can spot a bargain at a hundred paces but will only deem something to be worthy of purchase if it also meets quality control standards and is within their budget.

The concept of a budget is attractive to Cancerians who see this in itself as a form of security blanket. They see an evening spent working out the budget as being an investment and will carefully keep all receipts making regular checks to ensure that the budget is practical and working. In negotiation, Cancerians win through reticence. The person selling will think that Cancerian silence is due to over-pricing, but Cancerians are more likely to be wondering whether they need the product or not anyway. In pursuit of the sale, the seller then reduces the price and Cancerians, if they go ahead with the deal, get a bargain. It is not just in these reflective moments that Cancerians make headway, but also in their dialogue. Cancerians can be competitive and are not afraid of standing their ground and securing a fair price. They can barter and, except for the times when a treasured item is involved, can adopt a 'take it or leave it' stance. In this way, they secure superb deals.

It is Cancerians more than any other sign of the zodiac who respond to the idea of a 'nest egg'. With all the images of home security that this implies, the Cancerian hones in on the idea and as soon as possible will invest in a savings plan. The ideal savings plan may well be a protected mortgage such as a pension mortgage. If this is not applicable to them personally, then knowing that their savings are being invested in other property is comforting. Building Society schemes are popular for Cancerians. Even then, Cancerians will shop

around to get the best possible interest and will not be put off by having to commit their savings for set periods. Similarly, treasury bonds are attractive, simply because they appear to offer security.

Cancerians make excellent financial partners since they husband money so carefully. Their memories are sharp and their recall of the most intricate deal, intact. However, it must always be remembered that it is their security which is of primary interest. Any slip made by a financial partner which leaves the Cancerian position jeopardised will leave the relationship damaged. Cancerians must be able to trust other people's financial moves and, most importantly, have these explained succinctly at regular intervals. It is all too easy to undermine the Cancerian sense of security by unwittingly withholding information. When this is not a problem, Cancerians are strong partners whose financial instincts are reliable and unerringly honest. The Cancerian would never renege on a business expense budget and is more likely to astound partners by achieving deals at very little outlay.

As can be seen, with security playing such an important factor, Cancerians are not risk takers. Neither, however, are they boring investors. In fact, should they feel that they have sufficient knowledge to play the markets, they may well be tempted to do so. At the start, they may go for penny shares but, anxious to see return, they will follow the financial papers and probably invest in a newsletter so that they are sufficiently assured that they have made wise choices. It is more likely that they will sell when the shares have made significant profit for them, rather than wait until the market tops. In fact, they may have cause to reprove themselves more than once for having come out just before the real killing could have been made. It would be unthinkable for Cancerians to invest in any product which would be harmful to children, animals, the elderly or anyone in a vulnerable situation. On the contrary, they are attracted to those products which offer security to any of these. Having great interest in food themselves, it is not unlikely that they will be attracted to shares in food companies. Here though, they need to be familiar with the product. It is imperative to Cancerians to have an affinity with the goods before investing in them.

Some of the finest entrepreneurs are Cancerians. The blend of Cardinal and Water sign would seem to give excellent ingredients for 'get up and go' combined with instinct. In a sense, Cancerians are at their best when self-employed. In this situation, they can follow hunches and capitalise on their ability to combine administrative ability with creative flair. An asset for Cancerians is financial self-discipline. However, they also have a sizeable imagination and an intuitive understanding for the way in which a business has to operate if it is to succeed. Cancerians are neither work-shy nor financially illiterate. They are happy to invest in themselves by attending whatever courses seem appropriate but, more importantly, cultivate good relations with professionals who are likely to help them. Their weakness is their emotional instability. When knocked off this axis, their judgement is off key. Because of this, it is always wise for the Cancerian to have a sound family or emotional background from which to draw reserves during times of difficulty. With this in place, they readjust, realign, move their position a little and start their financial forward motion once more.

PRACTICE

1 Determine a minimum amount of cash that you feel comfortable carrying. Do not let yourself fall below this limit. Review this figure annually.

2 At the start of each month determine what you are hoarding either in cash or other items. Throw out what is unnecessary. Don't allow cash to stagnate.

3 Separate savings into two accounts. One for security and the other for holidays, etc.

4 Read at least one page of the financial section weekly.

5 Make friends with your bank manager. Agree an annual meeting.

6 Imagine being given a large sum. Half of it you can invest in a savings account. The other half has to be in shares. Choose which account and which shares you would use. Do this exercise regularly.

Leo

Those born under the sign of Leo are ruled by the Sun. Just as it is that the Sun is indispensable to life, so Leos feel that they too are indispensable. Leos value themselves highly and require that others acknowledge their value. Nowhere is this more obvious than in Leos' attitude to finance.

Leos know that they are valuable and are worthy of the best that is on offer. They are naturally attracted to the most expensive items on the shelves and require goods which 'shout' their quality and magnificence. Never are Leos more miserable than when they cannot afford a product. To be bereft of either cash or credit card to purchase an item is a painful experience indeed for those of this sign.

This being the case, it is strange that Leos do not learn to have more respect for cash than they do. One would suppose that they would treasure and store their money so that they could acquire goods as and when they need them. This, however, is not the case. Money quite literally slips through their fingers. This is not solely because Leos are busy purchasing items for themselves; commonly it is due to their enormous generosity towards others. As they themselves like to be appreciated with gifts, they enjoy showering others with abundance even if this compromises their own financial security.

What is important to Leos is how their cash is stored. It is as important to have a purse or wallet of good quality as to have

money inside it. The cash held within has got to look good too. Leos have a distaste for anything that looks scruffy or dirty. Notes should be new and coins especially should have a shiny quality about them. Foreign currency which looks and feels substantial has appeal for them. Alloy coinage with little weight is not something that they want to hold in their purse at all. On the other hand, a large and shiny coin that looks good and whose weight implies quality, feels very good to them indeed.

Leo is a Fire sign and those born under this sign have fiery impulses which they try very hard to keep under control. Should they become passionate about something then, until they have the object of their desire, they can be oblivious to all else. This can lead to difficulties in negotiation as, unlike other signs, they do not determine a bottom line figure of what they are prepared to pay for something before entering into negotiation. Blinded by the need to have the object, and unable to show detachment from what the outcome will be, they cannot help but make it clear to the seller that they are really interested. The experienced salesman can then drive a hard bargain and all too easily Leos can end up paying too much. Not that this will worry them. An inbuilt feeling of 'I deserved it' anyway gets them through any possible trauma. This is not to say that Leos are gullible. In fact, with Leo being a Fixed sign, they can display remarkable self-control. They then take great pride in their self-restraint.

Leos hate to be in debt to anyone – and the possibility of financial embarrassment is abhorrent. They may not see the use of credit cards as being debt and will enjoy having the more ostentatious of these cards available for use. But this, of course, requires that they keep a weather eye on their credit limit. All too often Leos are within 10 per cent of their credit limit and it is important that they manage to stay on the right side and experience no public humiliation at being shown to be on the wrong side of that limit.

Leos can save and enjoy thrifty saving habits but, as with all the Fire signs, the target figure must be both visible and attainable within a relatively short period of time. This group are not long term savers by nature. Like the other Fire signs, they do not like the idea of

being excluded from a savings plan by not meeting the initial conditions for entry. Long-term planning is unappealing to them and they resist attempts by bankers and accountants to get them to think seriously in this way. Where they excel, however, is in mastering the art of budgeting. This is anything but a natural skill for them but it is a concept that they are able to respond to and once the standing order is set up for them to have a chunk of money sent off to a savings account every month, a behaviour pattern is set up that proves invaluable. Their pride in this achievement is considerable.

Leos work well when they have a routine to stick to. On occasion, others can find this commitment tantamount to sheer obstinacy or stubbornness. However, it is the very routine of setting up and adhering to a savings scheme that benefits Leos and enables them to save up for items that they deem essential; usually holidays.

Financial partnership for Leos can be uneasy. It is imperative that the other party understands that what they may see as non-essential, Leos sees as essential. Indeed, much of what Leos do can seem extravagant to others. Under closer examination, however, it may be found that some of these apparent extravagancies have proved to be wise investments. Their ebullient nature and apparent confidence in the strength of their financial reserves when the reality is quite different, will exasperate the financial partner who has to try to deal with the newly created problem. Harsh words may be necessary but, even then, Leos may win by convincing the partner that only by conveying an image of wealth can wealth be attracted.

Leos are drawn to those things which are thought precious. They have an affinity with gold but other precious metals and jewels excite them also. They are natural speculators who have the happy knack of being able to buy at optimum moments and to see the value of goods rise spectacularly. They like nothing better than to be in the midst of an unfolding drama which sees them as central characters of the play. In one sense, play it is, since it is the thrill of being there, following the scent and making the final pounce just as the market seems to have stopped reacting that gives them a real thrill. The absurdity of it all and knowledge of having made a spectacular gain with little effort gives them much to smile about.

For Leos it is essential to have genuine enthusiasm for a stock before purchase. Poring over company accounts or newspaper tips can bore them rigid but they respond fast to someone's verbal tip. They have the ability to stay the course and to hold on to stock for a period of time. They want to see fast results but equally know that there is virtue in being steadfast. Persistence can pay off. In the case of Leos, this may be seen in the purchase of blue chip stocks which seem to have lost value but which they know will return to former glory. They have to take care here and be sure that they are holding on because their instinct tells them to and not because they need to be seen to be right.

When picking stocks, this group are likely to choose a somewhat diverse portfolio. They need to have some blue chip stocks but they also need to be able to illustrate their flair for taking the genuine risk. In this, they would seem to be drawn toward leisure or entertainment stocks. They are not averse to behaving as 'angels' and backing new films or to buying stocks in young entertainment companies. As long as they feel that an idea has credibility, they are willing to take a chance. Their diversity may lead others to view them as Super-traders who think big, think long term and think positive and thus gain results.

Leos have no problem whatsoever in self-investment. As naturally creative individuals, they have no problem in coming up with ideas. In fact, their greatest problem can be having too many ideas on the go at any one time. Their creativity, however, is fuelled by feeling good and that, in itself, may require that they buy themselves something to gain that feeling. Once they feel good, they also feel invincible and are convinced that any entrpreneurial idea will work and will work well. Being their own boss and having others working for them feels wonderful to this group. Having the title of Managing Director or President is better still. Whether the business be in its infancy or well established, Leo entrepreneurs require grandeur. As Leos naturally think big, they have no difficulty portraying themselves as the best there is. In this way, success is conveyed and further success assured.

PRACTICE

1 Have two purses or wallets. Associate one with feeling affluent and use the other to remind you of living within budget.

2 Develop an eye for a bargain. Window shop in all the best stores but only purchase in the last few days of their sales. Make friends with the assistants.

3 Test yourself frequently on interest rates. Know what the rate is for using your credit card and what rate you get on savings.

4 Keep a note of your weekly or monthly budget in your wallet. Look at this regularly.

5 Make friends with your financial advisor and arrange to meet for a coffee every few months.

6 Imagine if you had backed the latest film. Now think of ways to have something available to invest in a film in two years' time. Friends could give you something toward this fund for birthdays.

VIRGO

Virgo is the sixth sign of the zodiac and is an Earth sign. It is said that Virgos are perfectionists. This is perhaps an exaggeration. Virgos have an innate understanding that for anything to run smoothly, the details have to be correct. Reliable routines are therefore essential for Virgos. From this secure base, they are then able to use considerable analytical skill to test their system thoroughly and adapt it as necessary. Little distresses Virgos more than having doubt as to reliability; whether that be of a person or an object. It is essential for Virgos to have sound organisation so that they are able to adjust to what life throws at them. From the simple security of knowing exactly where the umbrella is for when it is raining, to the more complex security of a critical illness insurance policy that is guaranteed to provide sufficient funds if needed, Virgos have systems in place to cover as many eventualities as they can imagine. Even then, Virgos are quite capable of worrying endlessly over some imaginary crisis and how they would be able to cope with it. The truth is that the Virgo brain is able to juggle sound, practical reasoning with the numerous possibilities for solution to any problem and to develop a plan which is sufficiently adaptable to take into account conditions as they develop.

Security for Virgos lies in solid routine and this is as apparent in their attitude to finance as it is elsewhere in their lives. Quite early on in life, Virgos develop habits which stay with them throughout. From their earliest encounters with cash, they realise that it is a tool that may have a multitude of uses. To make best use of these, they need to monitor and control it well. Virgos then, husband their cash in ways unlike any other sign of the zodiac. There is something pleasurable about keeping notes of different denominations grouped together and similarly having containers for different units of currency. Notes or bills may be folded in one particular style from which they never deviate. It would be unthinkable for Virgos to have foreign currency mixed up with their own national currency and one could be assured that their purses or wallets would be streamlined in such a way as to ensure that different currencies or even coins of different value could not become mixed up. Virgos can demand so much of themselves that they have been known to make mountains out of molehills. When it is a financial mountain, they make it

sound like Everest. The reality is that matters are never quite as bad as they imply and once they have taken a deep breath and regained control of themselves, they soon find that they can reorganise, re-budget and, before long, be back on course.

Virgos attitude to credit card usage is controlled. It is not that Virgos do not have occasional lapses of self-control, but that even that loss of control is budgeted for. Should they exceed their personally determined limit, they readjust their spending for the next few months until the balance sheet is in order once more. Unlike many other signs of the zodiac, Virgos are well aware of how much they owe and to which card. Interest free credit arrangements are only undertaken when they are confident that they will be able to make the payments with ease. Virgos do not take unnecessary risks and are at their best when working within, and to, a set budget.

It is important for Virgos to have a savings plan set up. They see this as a contract between themselves and the managing firm and will question the rules and regulations governing the account before entering into commitment. Saving is essential for those of this sign. For Virgos, saving is a form of insurance against problems which may present themselves sometime in the future. It would also be unthinkable for Virgos not to consider both a pension plan and private health care. In the case of both of these plans, however, Virgos know that investment is not just in taking out cover, but also in developing a routine which safeguards against potential future difficulties. For this reason, Virgos tend to spend more than other signs both on health products but also on items which will prolong the life of objects in their care. The 'stitch in time' philosophy works well for Virgos. In spending, they take time and care to research the quality of the goods they are buying and any guarantees which are offered.

It is possible to come to the conclusion that Virgos would make perfect financial partners – but this is very rarely the case. They are excellent at auditing and controlling expenditure but it is quite possible that they are overly concerned with the detail and fail to grasp the bigger picture. In fact, Virgos become quite exasperated with those who talk about acorns and oaks. For them, that process can never be hurried and there will be enough time to appreciate the

oak once it is in front of them. Those who dwell in the realm of imagination or grand visions are more than just a little irritating to Virgos. It is also possible that others will see Virgo financial partners as being nit-picking, hyper-critical and fussy. That said, there are few business people who would not appreciate having a Virgo on their financial team. From credit control, to audit, to purchase manager, accountant or Finance Director, those of this sign are not afraid to look at realities and to present these clearly and regularly.

Facts are the rocks upon which all decisions are taken and Virgos have no problem in demanding accurate information from those with whom they wish to do business. Virgos may lack finesse, cunning or a capacity for deceit, but they are quite capable of negotiating using just hard facts and agreeing a deal that is adjusted for any flaw, is time controlled and has penalty clauses built in. Their arguments are controlled, the facts thoroughly researched and the Virgo manner direct and to the point. This can be quite disarming. They are as economical with time as they are with words so that negotiations are brought to a conclusion swiftly. That probably won't stop Virgos worrying as to whether or not they got the best deal and they may need to be reminded regularly that they always do the best for the time and for the situation as it was presented.

Playing the stock market is very much an intellectual exercise for Virgos. They make fine technical analysts and not only work hard to gain information, but check their sources thoroughly. Virgos can go for long-term play and are adept at gauging how much time it might be before they see major results. They may be drawn to bio-technical stocks, computer stocks, anything connected with the health industry and commodities. In each of these cases, they have an affinity with the product and have no difficulty in assessing what is likely to be at a premium and when. Virgos recognise the value of service and are attracted to those companies which service a regular need and which have a proven track record. These stocks will form the backbone to their portfolio. Nor are Virgos averse to the idea of going to the company Annual General Meeting. Virgos need to know what is going on and feel that it is better to hear accounts direct from the management than from journalists' reporting.

To be entrepreneurial requires courage, flair, imagination and a certain degree of workaholism. Virgos could never be accused of not working hard or long enough and have an ability to stay the course. Nor could it be said that they do not have flair. Their presentations are usually superb. They are in tune with the concept of service and would find it unthinkable not to fulfil commitments. In this sense they are excellent managers. However, they are not always good leaders and their tendency to keep imagination firmly under control may prohibit them from taking a risk and backing an idea. That said, if they feel that they have support from other professionals and their risk analysis shows good odds, they are able to set up their business and have it running efficiently in a relatively short time. If there are problems, they come from an apparent inability to take risks and to seize an opportunity as it presents itself. Taking time to run all necessary checks can also mean that the moment is lost. Their business is unlikely to fold through lack of imagination or risk taking, but growth will be slow albeit sure.

pRACTICe

1 Set aside some money for a 'fun' budget.
2 Use this money to buy 'penny shares' in new companies.
3 Reduce the amount of financial advice you take. Two or three sources should be enough.
4 Imagine that you are given a legacy but the terms are that you have to spend the money today. This will develop your decision making ability.
5 Give yourself a birthday gift of money to spend on something non-essential but which will make you feel rich.
6 Read one book a year about an entrepreneur who has taken high risks.

LIBRA

It is very easy for Librans to think that money is dirty, filthy, lucre. There is something not quite pleasant both about handling money and giving due consideration as to whether one has enough of it or not. Librans would like to be above such matters and prefer to adopt a rather disdainful attitude to personal financial matters. This is not to say that Librans are not capable of looking after financial affairs. Indeed this sign, symbolised by the scales, may be perfect at balancing the books and bringing creative flair to financial management. This does not alter the fact, however, that Librans generally do not like to handle cash, finding it onerous and dirty. There is something rather ugly about the whole idea of cash transaction to Librans whose interest may be maintained only when the notes and/or coins offered are freshly minted or artistically pleasing. For the rest of the time, they would prefer to keep some distance from actual cash. It helps, of course, for cash to be kept in an aesthetically pleasing container and for this reason, Librans make a wise investment when they purchase a good quality purse or wallet. Once cash is held within something that looks nice, they become more interested in looking after it.

Credit card transactions appeal far more to Librans who can generally maintain greater control of their finances by having regular summaries of transactions and statements to reconcile. In fact, it is this system that supports monthly budgeting. Librans are subject to quite violent mood swings. They experience enormous highs which are counter balanced

by extreme lows. Should the lows be caused by financial troubles, they will feel out of sorts for as long as it takes to get their finances back in order. As they grow older, the value of keeping their finances on an even keel and therefore averting these awful depressions becomes more and more important to them. They show great interest in how others resolve financial dilemmas and, unlike many signs of the zodiac, can learn from others' experiences. In time, they become very well adjusted indeed, particularly with regard to finances.

Haggling over price is quite alien to Librans. Their perception is that there is something a little vulgar about any kind of financial negotiation and that financial deals have to be undertaken in the most pleasing of settings. Bartering in a street market would appear unseemly to those of this sign unless this were done in a sufficiently good humoured manner. If shouting or haggling is involved they would as soon walk away from the deal. Librans are refined by nature and set great store by good manners. They may be competitive underneath that well-mannered refinement, but they are not about to enter into any dialogue that might border on a dispute in public.

It is in childhood when many saving and spending habits are ingrained. From a saving point of view, Librans like all those little games that make saving fun: the piggy bank, the Disney World bank account, etc. Librans tends to develop taste – usually rather expensive – rather early on. It seems that there is always some item that they believe will truly transform their existence. Acquiring this becomes a driving force and they will scrimp and save in order to make the purchase. It would be rare indeed for any Libra to build up vast financial reserves for there is always something that they feel they need to buy and which they feel would make their lives just a little easier. For those of this sign, the necessities of life include many items that others would consider to be luxurious. Librans do not suffer from a poverty stricken consciousness and fantasise about times when they will be able to afford all that they would like. When thinking about expected windfalls, it is all too easy for them to spend these several times over. Reading of the financial exploits of others never fails to amuse Librans and can whet their own appetite for trying out new spending and/or saving ideas. For a savings plan to

work for this group, it has to capture their imagination. The plans which work best will be those which demand that funds are 'locked up' for set periods of time, since this will stop them from emptying their savings for some purchase or other which they suddenly feel to be essential. Since environment is important to Librans, the bank or building society will have to be a place that they enjoy visiting. If it is untidy, unwelcoming, dirty or plain ugly, they will avoid visiting. Relating is crucial to Librans. Building up a rapport with a cashier or manager is another way of securing their financial position. They will usually honour advice given by someone that they perceive to be a friend. They are far less likely to respond to a mail-shot. The planet Saturn is exalted in the sign of Libra. Saturn is the planet associated with old age. So it is that Librans are aware that they will want to maintain a particular standard of living in their old age and will be happy to contribute to a pension scheme.

Part of the Libra quest in life is to find partnership. Once in a relationship they feel truly themselves. This is true in financial partnerships too. Librans are never short of a creative idea and these are usually both imaginative and up to the moment. Having a partner who can harness these financial ideas and align these with firm underpinning makes for a superb working partnership which can build success on success. Librans have a tendency to be swayed from the original objective by some fresh train of thought and this can be damaging. A partner who anchors them is essential. Librans contribute enthusiastically to a particular project and delight, with a partner, when the goal is achieved. A financial partner should not be confused with a romantic partner. It is not necessary for the two to go hand-in-hand.

As another of the information gathering signs of the zodiac, it is hardly surprising that those of this sign take pride in reading either the financial pages or otherwise gathering information about companies in which they have interest. Again, since they make sure that they have up-to-the-minute information available, they are able to adapt their portfolios constantly. However, being a sign not noted

for expending tremendous energy, they may be too lazy to take action on the information available and thus miss opportunities. As would be expected from those whose sign is that of the scales, Librans go for a well-balanced portfolio. Displaying all the traits of a Super-trader willing to speculate in the most outrageous market conditions, they balance these with conservative stocks which are generally blue chip. As a rule they are discreet in their trading, preferring as always to undertake their trades in a place of refinement. Good manners matter as much as good deals and one cannot proceed without the other.

Librans are keen to explore new ideas and unafraid of displaying leadership skills. They excel in self-investment with the result that many entrepreneurs may be found born under this sign. They are never short of ideas and their charm is such that they have little difficulty in persuading others to back their project. They may display grit and determination and can paint a good picture of exactly what it is that they would like to achieve and qualify the time frame that they have in mind. They do not compromise on spending to acquire information whether this be through books, study courses or consultants reports. In each case, they see the acquisition of information as being potential building blocks on the way to securing what they want. Their bankers may disagree and suggest that they follow bank guidelines alone, but Librans understand that in order to make good decisions, an all-round view must be taken. To this end, they will discuss with a variety of experts before making a final judgement. Never is this more true than in making financial judgements. Arriving at decisions in this area requires that Librans access all possible points of view and weigh these up carefully. Librans are all too well aware that once the decision has been taken, they are unlikely to want to review it. Just thinking about the effort that would be involved exhausts them! At such times, others discover the iron fist in the velvet glove of the Libra. With their sights set, decisions made and accurate information to sustain them, they reach their objective and fulfil their financial goal.

PRACTICE

1 Have a pleasing container to keep coins in. Empty your purse/pocket each day and save a particular kind of coin in this container. Empty it only on your birthday.
2 Invest this cash, but invest it in either Premium Bonds or small shares.
3 Your sign has an affinity with the planet Venus. Friday is Venus' day. Wait until Fridays to buy luxury items. You may find that you would have bought on a whim otherwise.
4 Commit yourself to a savings plan with a friend. Agree that this fund is not touched for five years.
5 Think of a minimum figure that is realistic for your current account. Do not allow yourself to 'overdraw' on this figure.
6 Make your financial advisor aware of your artistic leanings. Let your advisor know that you would be interested in investing in the arts whenever you can. Let them call you with ideas regularly.

SCORPIO

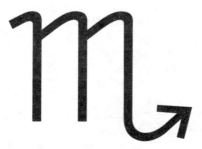

Scorpios are, perhaps, the most financially astute of the zodiac. As a Water sign, they are intuitive. But Scorpios also have determination. Together, these qualities result in them being well-equipped to develop a hunch, to back it and to stay with it. Scorpios are also the

great watchers and waiters of the world. They have no need to rush in to situations quickly and are quite happy to let events take their course and to bide their time before becoming involved. Involvement to Scorpios is never less than total commitment. They may appear to be sitting on the fence for a long time, but once they choose on which side to fall, they throw themselves wholeheartedly into a project. Scorpios and finance are well suited. If they decide to become fully involved here, their commitment verges on zeal showing themselves to be masters of the market place.

All this starts very early in life and usually at a point not long after their first experience of being short changed or cheated. Their resolution to never let that happen again becomes grim determination. Having experienced powerlessness once, they vow never to let it happen again. Whatever the circumstances might have been, Scorpios learn through experience to keep knowledge of their financial situation to themselves. No one will be able to violate this area of their life again. Of course, this then requires that they take more than a little interest in money generally. To Scorpios, knowing exactly how much cash they are carrying is vitally important. They also need to know the exact denomination of coins or notes involved. That way, they will be able to make all necessary checks and will be quick to notice any shortfall. Cash holds enormous fascination throughout their lives. They like the feel of it and even more, the power that having it can bring. Cash has to be kept safely and securely – and perhaps not all in one place so that the risk of it being lost or stolen is well spread. Scorpios are not mean but prefer to bring forth cash from a pocket or open their wallet well away from prying eyes. Notes or bills are secreted carefully by them. They fold them in all sorts of ways so that they and they alone know their value. They are suspicious of new notes – which may be fraudulent – and alien currencies. The familiar, tried and trusted is all important to those of this group. They prefer an old, well-worn wallet or purse to a new one and have set routines as to what should go into which pocket. Credit cards are really useful to Scorpios, offering as they do privacy as to a person's wealth and credit rating. When using their card, Scorpios are unlikely to make a public display of doing so and will prefer to tend the card upside down thus minimising the risk of others knowing which bank and

which card it is that they are using. Scorpios are unlikely to run up great bills and may, in fact, prefer the Debit Card system where you can only draw on available funds.

Thrifty by nature and unlikely to spend money without good reason, they will ask themselves the three big questions before purchasing anything. 'Do I need this?', 'Do I really need this?' and finally, 'Do I really, really need this?'. If a purchase passes all these tests then you can be assured that the Scorpio deems the purchase to have *real* value. Even then, Scorpios indulge their negotiating skills before making the final deal. Scorpios need to know what the bottom line value is of any product. They do not buy new if old will suffice and have a gift for being able to regenerate old or ill-used items. In negotiation they read the body language of the seller and gain a fair idea of what the cash value of an item really is. As buyers, their quiet, thoughtful and considered repose might even suggest disinterest in the product. But Scorpios are clever, knowing exactly when to turn away and when to turn back to make a bottom line offer. If haggling should become necessary, then Scorpios present a firm and considered argument that is hard to challenge. They are not put off if the dialogue becomes loud or ugly and can pursue their goal to the end. The net result is a superb deal.

Trust may be a small word in print, but for Scorpios it is a very large word indeed. Scorpios know their own weaknesses and can identify weakness in others. They know that working in partnership can give them strength. They may be drawn toward a person and feel instinctively that that person has all the right qualities; trust and integrity being essential. When this happens, they form a relationship at great speed. That speed works in the other direction as well, however. If the person lets them down they will sever all connections, with immediate effect. They will also ensure that they are adequately recompensed for any trouble or costs incurred. Scorpios are not free with information and partners will have to come to terms with apparent reticence. Their reward, however, will be in having a financial partner whose judgement is at times breathtaking.

It is apparent that Scorpios build up a certain amount of wealth given that their spending habits verge almost on the frugal and that they never pay more than absolutely necessary for anything.

Although they enjoying storing cash and having it safely around them, they do eventually require the services of a bank or building society for their savings. In making their choice, they weigh up what is on offer very carefully indeed. They are unlikely to be attracted by popular appeal savings accounts and will, instead, want to check what the past track record of a savings account has been. Unlike many other savers, they also want to know where the bank or building society is placing their investments. They do not tolerate mistakes with their account and demand excellent service. Spreading the risk and having more than one account may be an idea that they toy with but, generally, once they are happy with a set up they prefer to leave things as they are.

Scorpios are attracted to the idea of investing in others. Share options and venture capital have great appeal and here they show themselves to be super-sleuths. Scorpios are avid readers of stock prices and financial papers. They know that knowledge combined with instinct gives them a formidable lead over others. They have a nose for buying in at the bottom of the market. Unfortunately, they quite often sell before the market reaches its top since Scorpios never allow themselves to think that the market will go *that* high. They understand that it can go very, very low and never believe those who say that a stock is going to break the equivalent of its sound barrier. Nevertheless, Scorpios make shrewd market investors. They do not shrink from a product just because it seems socially unacceptable. They are attracted to stocks that others might ignore – environmental clean-up products, research stocks, weapons, etc. So it is that Scorpios can make a fast buck in areas that others often ignore.

Scorpios know that it is important to make provision for old age but do not necessarily believe that pension funds are the only way of doing this. Aware as they are that the market can go down as well as up, they choose to spread their investment in non-capital areas. They determine that it will be just as important to know how to protect oneself and to grow one's own vegetables as to have money in the bank and so will invest in areas a long way from finance but which offer basic security. Nor should it be forgotten that Scorpios are excellent collectors and invest large chunks of capital in collector's pieces. They will travel miles to track down another piece

for their collection and end up with an investment that few would appreciate fully but which in time proves to be priceless.

Underneath a calm exterior, Scorpios are in turmoil as to whether or not they are doing the right thing if they decide to go it alone in business. Really, they need a partner who can share the burden with them. However, it is not easy for them to share power. They do not have difficulty in investing some of their capital in a project of their own but a partner who wants to spend some money on, even apparently basic, materials like headed paper, may be seen to be a spendthrift. Scorpios are so very cautious in the way that money is spent that they squander little and make do whenever possible. They sell themselves and they sell themselves well. They work long and arduously and invest considerable time and effort in getting their business off the ground. In this they are usually very successful indeed. Their shrewdness and prudence will see their business turning a profit in a short time. They are also empire builders. They have no problem with buying an apparently defunct business and restoring it to life and, as such, are rather like company doctors. Others might think that any 'surgery' was unkind and cruel, but will soon see the newly revised business thriving on its new, lean skeleton.

PRACTICE

1 Spend an evening looking through cupboards. What have proved to be your best 'buys' and what did you pay for them. Compare relative price and quality.
2 Although you save well, has your money got 'stuck'? Keep your accounts active.
3 Invest in yourself. Money spent on your wellbeing is not necessarily wasteful.
4 Practise getting ready to broaden your portfolio. Read about foreign companies and determine which commodities you would like to invest in. Make friends with a financial advisor you can discuss ideas with.
5 Determine an annual budget. Work out a percentage of earnings that you can afford to invest.
6 On your birthday each year, compare your budget with the previous year. Be ready to *change* your budget system.

Sagittarius

Sagittarians long for the day when they will live in the land of plenty and that means a plentiful money supply as well as other riches. With Sagittarians everything is always possible and the odds rarely too high. Sagittarians are happy to purchase lottery tickets for any number of good causes and will never forget to check their numbers in case this time 'their ship has come in'. This is not to say that they are simply wishful thinkers. Sagittarians work hard for an honest day's pay and it would not occur to them to cheat on a deal. Money is something to be honoured and used. The latter aspect is important. For Sagittarians, money has to be kept moving. When stuck in one place for too long a time, it is as though the money itself forgets what it is there for. So it is for Sagittarians that cash is used and used. Within this circuit it seems that a vibration is set up so that money swirls around and around Sagittarians. They may feel that they never have enough of it but they certainly keep it moving.

Sagittarians like substance and so the feel of a wad of cash is exhilarating for them. Less so a handful of small change perhaps, but a feeling of plenty still exists so long as some cash is available. When Sagittarians have cash, it is brought out often. They are rarely mean and will give something to anyone in need. They appear familiar with a law of abundance that demands that as long as there is free flow of riches, the cycle will continue unbroken and riches will be brought back to them. Neither do Sagittarians fear using foreign currency. In fact, there is almost an air of excitement as they

become familiar with what this particular cash is capable of doing or not doing. Sagittarians will be aware of the exchange rate at the start of their journey but soon adapt to the different measure of currency on arrival. Thinking in new units is no problem at all.

Sagittarians enjoy spending and particularly spending which is associated with acquisition of knowledge. This, to them, is money well spent and rarely do they question the price involved. Negotiating is sport to Sagittarians but as a sport it can only be undertaken when they are fully prepared for the contest. Sagittarians do not barter naturally or negotiate easily but they are successful in this area when they are primed for the task and have researched prices and costs thoroughly. They will argue a point firmly and with authority but show grace when they have to concede a point to the other side. They have confidence that a deal will be reached and this is accomplished with neither side losing too much face. Sagittarians are not, therefore, the most skilled negotiators but neither are they weak in bartering skills.

It is not at all hard for Sagittarians to think big. They are not intimidated by big business or left in awe of banking authorities. They feel excluded from nothing and expect to have honest dialogue with persons whose word, as their own, is 'as good as their bond'. Sagittarians value professionals. They have no wish to understand the intricacies of professional financial management and only wish to be assured security, and that the person handling their finances is doing so with integrity. Rarely do Sagittarians spend time studying the various savings plans on offer, preferring to make their choice instead through expediency. If the bank is long established, the rate is good and the procedure simple enough, they go ahead with the plan. Sagittarians are generally bored by talk of investment portfolios and will run a mile from any aggressive selling. Given that they live for the moment, talk about the long-term future is both tedious and frustrating. This is not to say that they are unwilling to set up a regular standing order from current to savings account; rather that they need to do this from their own initiative and not that of some advisor. The salesperson who can persuade them that it was really their own idea in the first place will do well. This sort of regular saving works well for Sagittarians when coupled with just one annual

review of the fixed amount to be involved. It should be remembered that Sagittarians have no intention of sitting on a nest egg for any length of time. They are happy to save up for a specific purpose and then to deplete reserves and start all over again. They have no need to accrue funds just because that is the norm. What they do need to know is that they will be able to access money when they need it; and that means building some reserves alongside good credit rating.

Sagittarians prefer to use cash whenever possible. If they are obliged to use credit cards then they want to pay the bill off quickly. Financial partners should remember this and govern joint finances accordingly. Sagittarians do not work well with those who run up large debts. Sagittarians may be large spenders but generally they keep within their means. They do not respond at all well to large burdens of debt and, in fact, will feel these as though they are millstones. Perhaps it is because they are so aware of this trait that they prefer debit to credit cards. This acts as a brake on their spending which might otherwise be subject to no restraint whatsoever.

It is not true that Sagittarians are luckier than any other sign of the zodiac but it is probably the case that they come out on top as often as they lose out. Along the way, they will have been exhilarated by the risks that they have taken. Having a partner who can curb their propensity to gamble rather more than they ought can be beneficial. Sagittarians do not make wonderful ledger keepers and benefit greatly when someone else is keeping an eye on day-to-day costs. Sagittarians do, however, think fast and can seize a bargain whilst others are working out whether or not they can or should go ahead with the deal.

It is this trait which makes them fine stock market players. Their ability to make quick decisions, combined with sure knowledge of the odds, results in them being able to select a good buy and to get into the frame before others have even seen the opportunity. Once the stock is bought, they are able to read all the signals and sell just as the market tops. Occasionally this backfires – when they were just a shade too rash – but Sagittarians can shrug these errors off and move on to the next thing with little angst being shown. All told, they are good traders, their social skills being such that they mix with many and acquire titbits of information that they can use to

their advantage. It is acquisition of information that forms much of their market playing strategy. That, and backing an instinct or hunch, pays off more often than not. Sagittarians are not necessarily attracted to the biggest players in the market place. Neither will blue chip companies warrant too much attention. Where Sagittarians excel as forward thinkers, is in picking stocks whose time is about to come. The stocks may vary from penny shares to commodities; either way it is an acute sense of timing that leaves them mainly winners in the market place.

As entrepreneurs Sagittarians have a major problem in that they are not attuned to the nitty gritty of daily business life. Paperwork is not for them and in fact becomes a chore that they do not handle well. It is all too easy for them to fail to record a business transaction correctly so that the auditor/accountant is left with quite a mess at the end of the financial year. That said, Sagittarians evolve some wonderfully creative propositions which have enormous potential. With the right deputies in place, these ideas can be fully realised. Without these, the ideas may never quite get off the ground. Positively, Sagittarians are never limited by the immediate horizon. Their ability to think on a grand scale and to assume that most problems can be overcome are also assets. Sagittarians have no interest in power but do like to be seen to have 'backed the right horse'. Part of their learning curve is the discovery that with fulfilled ideas comes authority and recognition ; maintaining this pace can be difficult. With just a modicum of attention to detail and utilising their broadening wealth of experience, they can realise many more ambitions and enjoy extraordinary productivity with consequent financial success.

PRACTICE

1 Practise knowing how much cash you have at any time. Test yourself frequently.
2 Set yourself a monthly budget for reading material. Live within the budget.
3 Open an extra savings account. Put aside 10 per cent of your other savings into this account. Promise yourself not to touch this account for five years.
4 Choose a 'fantasy' portfolio using 5000 pounds or dollars make-believe money. Check the status of this portfolio weekly.
5 Find a folder, an old shoe box or file and put receipts into this one place.
6 Set aside one day a year, a month before your birthday, to review your financial affairs. Mark this in your diary.

CAPRICORN

Capricorns have a wonderful instinct for survival and it is important to them that what they build up during their lifetime is secured for generations to come. As a result, it is not at all unusual to find that they amass considerable wealth and that they achieve positions of considerable authority. In their desire to reach the top of the mountain of success, they are often seen to take up quite precarious positions *en*

route. Yet they are sure footed and rarely require assistance from elsewhere. Capricorns know exactly where it is that they have come from and where they are headed. They do not always take the most direct route and at times take risks that others find awe inspiring. Deeply ingrained within the Capricorn psyche is the idea that you only get out what you are prepared to put in to any task. They have no expectation that money will simply fall into their lap. Should it do so, they feel that it is incumbent upon them to take care of the windfall and to advance its value. These characteristics are displayed early on in their lives. They respond well to the idea that pocket money should be earned. Equally, they see that gifts of money should be spent wisely.

Capricorns enjoy the feel of cash. It acts as a padding or security blanket around them. One could be assured that if they had a cash empty wallet or purse, this would be made up for by plentiful credit cards. However, it is the feel of cash that warms them most – especially notes or bills of high denomination. Their purse or wallet is kept neatly with large denominations kept separately to ones of lower value. Their preference is for new, crisp notes. Respect for cash comes naturally to them and older notes and bills are smoothed out carefully to make them look as new. They do not however overlook coins of small value. Even these are treasured and perhaps even hoarded. They know that there will come a time when there are enough of them to exchange for a new note.

In their spending habits, Capricorns have their own quality-control management and are unlikely to make frivolous purchases. Others might be tempted to think that they are mean. This is not the case at all – it is simply that they are not at all wasteful, preferring to see themselves as thrifty. They do not just visit old, well established firms for their shopping but have a decided preference for those shops which show a commitment to long-term trade. This is a form of guarantee to Capricorns who need reassurance that someone will be there to assist them at a later date should the goods be found faulty. Capricorns purchase for the long-term and would prefer to save up for the best. This is not always practical and being practical matters to Capricorn. An expedient purchase will be one which meets practical requirements and which will retain some modicum of value. As the time approaches when they can afford to replace

the item with something of better quality, they will hope to regain some of their initial 'practical' investment.

Capricorns have a willingness to negotiate and accept that meetings and debate are necessary before most deals are struck. They are masters of time and can display extraordinary patience as they take up a position and then wait for the other party to respond. A grim determination comes over them as they await the next move in the game. For Capricorns, there is no need to hurry. 'All things come to those who wait'. Even in appalling conditions and under threat from elsewhere to get a deal signed quickly, they persist in negotiating until a reasonable and fair deal is struck. The fairness of a deal is important to them. They may well want to do business with the person again and need to know that both sides are comfortable with the exchange as a result. Manners are important here too. Capricorn behaves decorously and expects others to do the same. Deals are confirmed in writing and their word is their bond.

Saving is not at all a difficult concept to Capricorn. From an early age they respond to the idea of putting aside a proportion of their earnings. Saving, quite simply, feels better than spending. Nor do they need to have a particular objective in mind when they start a savings plan. It is just important to have started the scheme and to know that funds will be available as and when necessary. Setting up a standing order to transfer money from their current account to the savings account presents no problem whatsoever and in time, Capricorns will increase the amount involved. As in all things, regularity is important. Capricorns enjoy rhythms and patterns and it would be unthinkable for them to miss a payment unless absolutely necessary. Capricorns are attracted to the idea of National Savings or Bonds and are not troubled by the idea of having funds tied up for long periods of time. What this means, of course, is that Capricorns build up a considerable capital base which then offers the opportunity for them to make different types of investment later on.

It is not hard to see that Capricorns appear attractive as financial partners, particularly as they grow older. They become financially secure, prudent, astute but, most of all, willing to take the occasional risk which, to Capricorns, is actually an educated gamble. It is

important to remember that they are 'risk averse' as opposed to 'risk takers'. Their shrewdness demands that they assess a proposal with careful scrutiny. Should the Capricorn decide to go ahead with a deal, they will also have a time frame in mind and expect to see results by a set date. Should these not be forthcoming, the Capricorn will find a way to break free. Capricorns are drawn to action. They do not like to let life stagnate before them and where finance is concerned, get some thrill from taking a stance which others might see as precarious. This blend of conservative saver and venture capitalist may be hard for others to accept. In financial partnership they value those who comprehend the detail whilst maintaining hold of the long term vision. Even more, they are attracted to a partner who will bring ideas and opportunities to them. Capricorns tend not to mix with the really creative individuals who would benefit from their backing. Having a partner who can make the introductions is invaluable!

It is once their financial base is felt to be sufficiently secure that Capricorns join in the more exciting aspects of the financial world. Investment and, particularly, retirement planning comes naturally to Capricorns and they become interested in long-term savings and pension plans relatively early in life. Neither do they necessarily leave the management of their investment to others. As they grow in confidence, they want to manage their own portfolio. Once they have a rudimentary knowledge of how the market works, they are ready to sit down and study the indexes. Initially they will monitor the share prices of blue chip or well-established stocks and make investments in this area. Having a natural affinity with banking, it is probable that they would be drawn to stocks in this area. However, over time, this will not satisfy their craving to experience a little risk. Here, they either study a young company very carefully before investing or join venture capital schemes which are government approved and which offer tax advantages. This is another way of minimising the risk. Just occasionally however, Capricorns are persuaded to invest in a person who is a long way off from having their company quoted on the stock exchange. Should they take this route, you can be assured that the

Capricorn knows the individual very well and has great confidence in that person's ability to make headway.

Capricorns are often described as showing a wisdom beyond their years or at the very least as having old heads on young shoulders. It is hardly surprising then that entrepreneurial traits may be displayed at a relatively young age. With a tendency to convey an air of seriousness and/or authority, it is not hard for them to persuade others that their ideas are sound and that the other person should invest in the product or service. Capricorns do not have as much imagination as other signs and their product or service might be described by others as down to earth but reliable. They are unlikely to develop fancy packaging or to spend a fortune on public relations, advertising or marketing. Others would no doubt agree, however, that the Capricorn database is kept up to date, that they serve their customers well and that what they miss in finishing touches they more than make up for in pleasant and reliable dealing. Capricorns have total confidence in their ability to take the business from acorn to oak and little difficulty whatsoever in persuading others that this will be the case. Centred, as they are, on the long-term goal, they usually achieve it.

PRACTICE

1 Determine to buy one 'fun' item for every safe or quality item that you buy.
2 Find out more about your financial advisor. Does your advisor invest in anything artistic. If so, why? Could you do the same?
3 For your birthday each year, buy yourself a gift which reminds you of growing wealth.
4 Read one book a year about a company whose fortunes have been turned around through creative thinking.
5 Look out for a small company that you know has financial problems. See how you could help and ask for shares.
6 Open an extra account. Save money in this for risk taking ventures.

Aquarius

Aquarius is the last of the group of signs known as the Air group. It is a complex sign. Individuals born under this sign often seem to contradict themselves. Others may think that the words and actions of Aquarians are at variance with one another. Aquarians would abhor this comment since they know that they are always true to themselves. The problem is that for them every moment in life is different and has to be honoured accordingly. If this results in disparity in behaviour then so be it as far as Aquarians can see. They are an unusual group of people precisely because that is what they want to be. They may enjoy the intellectual exercise of analysing others but do not like it when others weigh up their actions and behaviour. Freedom and independence are essential characteristics of Aquarians and it would be anathema to them to concede that others are able to predict their behaviour. They have to be able to respond to the moment. However, they have a natural feel for the future and are often far ahead of their time. Life to them is made richer by new advances and ideas. All too easily they are exasperated by the past and frustrated by those whose behavioural patterns are built on historic and traditional approaches. They may have respect for that person's point of view, but require that others understand that they have to do things their own way too.

Whilst this may seem easy to understand, it masks something infinitely more complex. For, although Aquarians are looking ahead

to the future and demand the right to be able to behave in their own peculiarly unique, and occasionally eccentric, way, they are also egalitarians and humanitarians. They have no difficulty dealing with the idea that 'no man is an island' and they set great store by the need for people to work together, to look after those less able, for rich to share with poor. The problem for them is that one half accepts the need for rules, regulations and taxation whilst the other sees a rule as something that is meant to be broken and taxation as unfair. Mixing co-operative ideals with the right of every individual to do their own thing, inevitably brings them into conflict not just with themselves but also with authorities. The area of finance is just one platform where these conflicts are experienced and where they try so hard to find resolution – the resolution as often as not being unconventional and innovative.

As an Air sign, Aquarians have no difficulty in fantasising about money in whatever form. Money is, after all, simply a means to an end. The handling of cash requires the use of certain practical skills and that bores Aquarians rigid. Cash may require a container of some sort but Aquarians do not dwell on what form this container should take. Not for them the tiresome task of making sure that bills are folded in a certain way or that notes should even be kept separate to coins. Herewith lies a basic problem; the apparent lack of respect that Aquarians show towards cash masks a healthy respect for finance generally. Perhaps more than any other sign, Aquarians know what can be achieved when finance is available. They are shrewd shoppers, savers and investors but to display these traits requires that they invest in the necessary time to do essential research. This is something that they can only do when they are truly in the mood. At other times, their lack of interest means that they will simply tune out to any discussion about finance or related subjects. It is quite simply too tedious. Yet at other times, their savvy in this area can be outstanding. They may leave others totally confused; blowing hot and cold on financial matters. Their attitude is perhaps the most exasperating of any of the signs to the financial advisor who will not have a clue as to what reaction he/she is going to receive on any given day. One thing the advisor might care to remember is that Aquarians' attention span is short. They are quick

on the uptake and do not require to go into long involved discussions on anything quite so mundane as money. They want to set up a plan quickly and with the minimum fuss so that they can get back to what it is that really interests them.

The kind of savings plans which appeal to Aquarians are those where ethical considerations have been taken into account. Co-operative banking appeals to them but then so, too, does the idea of having a Merchant Bank account which is exclusive. Aquarians may need both in order to fulfil the two radically different parts of their make-up. Again, their savings pattern may go from one extreme to the other. They may save regularly for a while only to become bored with the game or have need of the ready funds. Then they have long periods when they do not save at all. This mirrors their spending habits generally. At one point they may spend, spend, spend and, at another time, control their spending to such a degree that others become concerned that they are trying to do without essentials. It is this proneness to extreme and exaggerated behaviour that makes it so very hard to suggest ways in which Aquarians may help themselves to build a more secure financial base. They may crave security but can all too easily sabotage any gains that they have made by making a sudden withdrawal and leaving themselves back at square one. Even elementary checking of their bank statement is too trifling or tedious for them. The real problem is that they can excel at budgeting and yet at other times show themselves to be total spendthrifts. They become bored by routine and almost have to do something to break out of what they perceive as a rut even if this means that they leave themselves financially vulnerable.

As a rule they do not make good financial partners for all the reasons given above. Their need to be free to do their own thing is so strong that it would be hard for anyone else to become closely involved with them. Aquarians would feel seriously threatened and undermined by someone sharing control of their finances. Trying to explain why they had taken certain actions or justifying an expense would seem just too, too irritating. Called upon to explain some financial action, they may display a degree of stubbornness and wilfulness that leaves others quite uncomprehending. Aquarians are indeed 'one-offs' and are at their best when allowed to go their own way.

This works exceedingly well for those Aquarians who are self-employed. They are creative individuals and have no problem with coming up with an idea to market. The idea is likely to have widespread appeal and to be something which improves the quality of life for others. Aquarians will offer a fair deal for a fair price and will have no difficulty in negotiating deals. Their ability to present reasoned argument comes to the fore and they can hold their own until a final agreement is reached.

Investing in themselves is something that Aquarians have to do anyway. Few others can understand what it is that they want to do and they are almost too futuristic themselves to be able to present their case to bank managers or venture capitalists. It is almost as though their vision of the future would be damaged by too much focus on practicalities or details. Preparation of a business plan may be intellectually stimulating – but not for long. Yes, it would be better if they gave these matters greater priority but it appears that, in doing so, their energy and enthusiasm for the project is somehow diminished. They are at their best when allowed to focus on the main aim and objective. They are more than capable of making it all happen and have no fear of investing capital, time and expertise until they have achieved their goal. There is no question that they will not pay employees a fair price. In all things, Aquarians strive to be true and kind. What all this means is that it may be some time before they have extra reserves with which they can then play the markets.

Initially, the stock and bond markets are alien places to Aquarians but, with their fast grasp of what is going on around them, it is not long before they understand the basic rules of the game and are ready to join in. Inevitably, Aquarians are attracted to those stocks where the product is futuristic. High-tech stocks usually appeal but their imagination is also captured by stocks which may not have moved for some time. Having acquired even just a little information, Aquarians are extraordinarily adept at sensing when the stock is ripe for a move and buying in at just that moment. The problem here is that the move may not necessarily be in an upward direction and there are all too many Aquarians who have had their fingers burnt by buying too much of a stock which has made a disastrous move downward. However, this is all part of life's rich tapestry for

Aquarians. They take such blows on the chin, rarely moan and always resolve to research a little better next time. Once they learn that their instinct is for the market move and that they will need further information at that point before they themselves react to this, they learn to make more informed and rather more rational decisions. Of course, saying that to them would turn them off entirely. Aquarians are not at all afraid of behaving irrationally and can recount instances when that natural quirkiness has paid off handsomely.

PRACTICE

1 Buy a good quality purse or wallet. It can be quite original but one that makes it difficult to 'stuff' notes into. Notes and bills need to be treated with respect.
2 Mark four random dates in the year in your diary for giving yourself a financial health check.
3 Visualise which bank you would like to have an account at if you were very rich.
4 Find out what the minimum figure is to open an account there.
5 Plan to reach this figure within a set period.
6 On your birthday every year, make sure you know your bank manager's name. Leave your best wishes for him.

Pisces

Pisceans need to go with the flow and assume that it will be moving in a positive direction. When it comes to finance, Pisceans assume that things can only get better. When their finances take a downward turn, they are confused. Piscean view of money is that it has magical properties. They are captivated in childhood by the deeds of the Tooth Fairy and the stories of King Midas or of flax being spun into gold. It is the legacy of these which leads them to believe that cash is special and that it is important always to have it available so that it can be 'spun' into more. It is, therefore, unnerving for them to experience it behaving in a non-magical way. Piscean imagination is such that they see money as a seamless flow of energy which transforms cash into goods and back over and over again. The concept of 'half a sixpence being better than none' is valid for Pisceans. They feel that this one half will attract the other half, sometimes taking this quite literally. They may have a lucky coin or token and deduce that this will look after other coins floating in the dark recesses of a pocket or wallet.

Pisceans have no need to know exactly how much cash they are carrying at any time. They have an understanding and belief that the cosmos will provide so that it does not seem to be important to them to know how much they have down to the last penny. An empty purse or wallet might worry them since they need to feel that they have enough for immediate needs but their belief system tells them that they will be provided for and that worry might create a negative force field which stops the flow of abundance. When they have cash they spend it – and not always wisely. To prevent this, they carefully fold bills or notes and put these away somewhere for a rainy day. As often as not however, they 'lose' touch with this money so that it is not unusual for them to come across it some considerable time later. When they do, it seems like an unexpected gift from the Gods.

Credit and debit cards are danger zones to Pisceans. There seems little magical about a piece of plastic that has not been minted in Midas' castle and, unable to identify with the plastic card, operating with it is extremely difficult. It is all too easy for Pisceans to adopt a somewhat careless approach so that debts mount up. In the end they may come to the conclusion that it is better not to have these cards at all to prevent falling into what they see as a trap.

Pisceans are generous and would never turn their back on someone in need. Rarely do they count the cost of this – far less budget for behaving in this way. Budgeting at all is not easy for them. To budget requires focus and planning and is, therefore, alien to those whose natural state is to go with the flow, trusting that somewhere along the line all will be well. In this, they are often fortunate. Pisceans have been known to have money luck through small windfalls. In the form of cash, this can go straight through their fingers. It is hard for them to take cash to the bank, preferring instead to have it around for when they might have need of it. If the cash is not too great an amount, they are likely to give others a treat and simply enjoy the moment. Larger sums cause them to stop and think. They may indeed take these to the bank but, should they do so, their imagination permits them to commit the money several times over. Spending money more than once is an all too common phenomenon for Pisceans.

This may suggest a weakness when it comes to handling money but there is no weakness apparent when they are negotiating. Pisceans can haggle par excellence and have no fear of telling a little white lie if it suits the occasion. They know what they are prepared to pay and may even sift through a stack of identical items to find one whose box is slightly damaged so that they can ask for some discount. They may well ask for discount for paying cash anyway. They do not do this because they are in any way mean – more because it is something of a game to them and yet another way in which the Gods can be shown to be looking after them.

Planning for the future through saving is not an easy concept for Pisceans. They like the idea of a sum of money invested coming out as something much larger at the end of the day but the reality of saving is hard. Short term saving may be relatively simple – putting aside money for a holiday or special meal but long-term saving requires something different. In the past, insurance policies provided an excellent way for Pisceans to save. Pisceans did not connect the monthly standing orders with a form of saving and honoured the contract to pay the set sum each month. There is no guarantee that such policies will offer the same return in the future, but some may still offer a savings method for Pisceans.

Pisceans are served well by partners who can curb their spending. They are quick to barter and may well have negotiated a sale or purchase in a matter of minutes. It may be open to question as to whether or not this was a good long-term move. Nevertheless partners will admire the imaginative way in which Pisces goes about business. It is never easy to keep track of all Pisces' financial machinations; as with so many things in their life, they dart in and out just like the fishes they are. This may cause the accountant to have a seizure, but Pisceans will cope with this too, offering sympathy and support, and promising to mend their ways and to keep accurate accounts in future. In reality, they will be desperate to slip away! Being stopped dead in their tracks and asked to account for everything is anathema to the fish.

The idea of gaining financial advancement through a lucky market move captivates Pisceans. They may long for the day when they have the kind of money that means that they can buy into the market. As with all gamblers, their first forays tend to be fortunate ones. The futures market appeals strongly to the Pisces imagination. Pisces being a Water sign, instincts are good at the start of their trading and they may well make a vast sum on an early trade. However, it seems that the more knowledge that they have, the more likely it is that they lose touch with their instinct. Decisions taken under these conditions could cause them to lose heavily. Where Pisceans make gains is in recognising a creative idea and following it. They are not overly worried as to how a particular company may or may not have done in the past, they simply get on the scent of the idea being presented at the time and, if it captures their imagination, back it.

As a Mutable sign, Pisceans lack some obvious leadership abilities in terms of get up and go, but this is more than made up for by an unerring instinct for what could be a profit-making idea. Neither business plans nor strategies work for Pisceans. They need to be free to follow their own hunches on a daily basis in their quest to turn cloth into gold. They are entrepreneurs of superior talent. Like 'theatre angels' who back a show, their hunches work and work well. In this way, they are fantastic self-investors. Their way of doing business may be a mystery to everyone else – and it may not even be possible for them to explain exactly what they are doing and why –

but it works. Pisceans set no limits on how far they or their finances can go. They cannot help but think big and in the long run usually achieve their vision.

PRACTICE

1 For your birthday, buy yourself a 'lucky coin' – but make this an old coin that is also a collector's piece.
2 Visit your bank once a week and deposit something – even a token amount.
3 Read one financial article or listen to a money programme each week.
4 Imagine that you had to invest a sum on someone else's behalf. What would you invest in. Do this exercise regularly.
5 Before you buy anything, ask yourself if you really need the product. Then if you really, really need it. And lastly if you really, really, really need it.
6 Have pictures of items that you are saving for prominently displayed. Don't allow yourself to forget what you are saving for.

4 YOUR FUTURE WEALTH

What we have seen so far in this book is that major factors in determining financial attitudes are the cycles of the outer planets, which form a generational influence, combined with the Sun-sign position which give more individual expression. It is in study of the former that we can begin to make some forecasts as to how each Sun sign is likely to benefit in the coming years.

The planet Pluto takes approximately 246 years to make its path around the zodiac. In 1996, Pluto began its long and stately journey through the sign of Sagittarius. Pluto is acknowledged to be the planet of birth and resurrection. It does not always have a negative effect, rather it demands that outmoded ways of being are pared away and new foundations sunk. However, the process can feel life threatening. Using the analogy of a young plant that is in the process of being repotted, we see that from the plant's perspective, being uprooted from a position where it initially thrived, can indeed seem treacherous. The fact is, however, that in repotting, the plant will experience new growth as a result of the benefits of the nutrients in the freshly prepared soil. As Pluto moves through each successive sign of the zodiac, it appears to create upheaval and considerable distress, but it also makes way for new growth and new developments.

Pluto, as ruler of the Underworld, is the God of Wealth. Life cannot survive without the nourishing vitamins and minerals from down below. The acquisition of these may cause much pain and anguish and considerable physical toil, but the end result is the unearthing of products which enrich our lives. Pluto is said to 'rule' the sign of Scorpio – in other words its effects are at their greatest as it moves

through that sign. It made its passage through Scorpio between 1983 and 1996. During this period we saw great upheavals in the Scorpionic business and financial world. Big business was called to account more than once and it was clear that new structures would have to be built. Corruption began to be unearthed and new ethical codes for investment started to gain ground. This was only the beginning. If Pluto's total journey time through the zodiac is 246 years, we should anticipate that it will take at least half of that cycle for Pluto to root out corruption and put in place strong, healthy, pure roots. The new foundations, standing sure on uncontaminated financial ground will be able to support new and large endeavours.

As Pluto makes its passage through Sagittarius – a journey that will take from the present period until 2008, we may expect crusades for moral or ethical investment to continue to make their presence felt. The uncovering of further corruption *en route* is likely and accountability will become a major issue. It is in the determination of what and who can be trusted that Pluto really plays its part. Sagittarius is the sign associated with foreign affairs and so it is likely to be that each country will have to call into question the integrity of its neighbours. Nowhere is this likely to be felt greater than in terms of currency.

What we might expect until 2008, is for seeds of disquiet as to the true value of currency to be sown. The capital reserves of each country will be called to account and those travelling will question, in a more detailed way, the value of cash currency used during their journey. All this is made more complex by the use of credit card transaction and the speed at which these are processed. Cases of fraud and major blips in the system could make life difficult indeed for the traveller.

Sun sign Sagittarians may well feel as though their wings have been clipped under these conditions. However, they will not be the only sign of the zodiac to experience problems during this time. The other mutable signs, Gemini, Virgo and Pisces will all find themselves having to tackle crises which are peculiarly finance orientated. Each in turn will have to find ever more creative ways of getting round the problem and each is likely to feel that their particular talents are not

working as well as they have in the past, and that they need to bring forth other talents to get around the difficulty. Geminis will find that there is a time when talking has to stop and that negotiating has a finite time limit imposed. They will have to learn the art of determining fixed value. Likewise Virgos will find that facts have become moving targets so that what applied at one point of time does not hold true a moment or so later. They will need to learn the art of making a fast deal based on the facts as they are presented at the time.

Where Gemini and Virgo are likely to find their wits tested to the full, Pisceans will find themselves working on a quite different problem. Pisceans are most likely to have direct experience of loss through fraud or through investments which do not return the kind of gains long hoped for. As the most adaptable sign of the zodiac they will no doubt work around this difficulty, but the effect of having to swim through financially polluted waters should not be underestimated. In their search for purity, the Pisces will have to travel through previously uncharted waters.

If Sagittarians experience the financial stuffing being knocked out of them, it will be through the discovery that currencies on which they relied and investments which they held to be good, are found to be corrupt and tainted in such a way that use of them is quite unacceptable. As we have seen, Sagittarians value morality and ethics above all else. Having to concede that those professionals who were looking after their investments have behaved with less than acceptable integrity will be shocking in itself. The process of rebuilding their financial security will not be easy and may require that they learn more about international investments than they thought they would ever want to know.

Of these four Mutable signs, both Virgo and Pisces are likely to respond to the upheavals best; Virgo because once they have understanding of the new world order at work, they will respond to that. Pisceans, who by nature can forgive almost anything, may not be happy with having to incorporate such fundamental changes, but it is their nature to adapt and adapt they will.

The sign least likely to be able to absorb changes in the nature of currency and money will be Cancer. Cancerians, for whom familiarity

is so important, will find the move into electronic currency quite unsettling. They may accept that some currencies are worthless and that the countries concerned have inadequate reserves but, they will think, if this is the case with currencies they have trusted, what of the others? It will be quite frightening for Cancerians to have to cope with new monetary systems and we should expect that it will be the Cancerians who demand of their governments that their monies are held secure and electronic frauds or other losses made good.

Almost as unsettled as the Cancerians will be the Taureans, for whom change is always a challenge. Unlike the Cancerians, however, Taureans will not be left feeling emotionally damaged by the changes and, instead, we may find that it is the Taureans who, having coped with enormous upheavals during the period between 1983 and 1996 and, now experienced in financial crisis, will demand that the new system meets their requirements. Indeed, it is to be hoped that Taureans will play a large role in new monetary exchange arrangements.

Aries, Leo, Libra, Scorpio, Capricorn and Aquarius will each, in their own way, adapt to new ways of working. Aries, Leo, Libra and Aquarius will enjoy the speed of fast transactions and once they are used to the new system will make it work for them. The Scorpios and Capricorns, who need rather longer to adapt, are likely to make financial gains during the period through exercising caution. It is these signs who are most likely to have reserves less vulnerable to change.

In May 2000 an extraordinary line-up of planets takes place (see p. 74). Jupiter and Saturn will once more be conjunct – this time in the Earth sign of Taurus. We know now that this cycle plays a major role in economics. Those cycles which began in 1900, 1920, 1940 and 1960 had a common theme – saving and building capital base before spending. Obtaining and using credit gained rapid popularity halfway through the 1960 cycle and by 1981 when the 'yuppie' age had dawned, there were many who thought little of getting themselves into debt through large mortgages, finance deals on cars and the use of credit cards. Having no capital base but able to show that their earnings would cover repayments meant that few people were excluded from being able to enjoy a relatively high standard of

living even though they lacked comfortable reserves from which to draw during times of trouble.

This applied to countries as well as to individuals, so that there are many countries in the world hugely indebted to others. The theory seemed good. Money was lent on the basis that it would be paid back over time and with considerable interest. The theory, however, was flawed in that it failed to take account of natural disasters. This caused untold suffering in some areas of the world and left those nations unable to repay even the interest on their loans. On an individual level in the West, the theory came unstuck for different reasons but with the result that lack of solid capital resource left some individuals effectively bankrupt or facing the problems of negative equity on their homes.

Against the backdrop of the 1981 Jupiter Saturn cycle which began in an 'Air' sign this can be understood. Economic ideas were grand in thought but poor in practicality. The large scale banking crashes seen since 1981 were probably inevitable. Investors wishing to withdraw their cash found insufficient capital reserves for them to do so. Combined with fraud and grandiose management schemes so far removed from the one owner – one company state, many institutions came to the point of collapse. One problem has been that of accountability. We have seen governments having to bail out failing banks and corporations whilst the International Monetary Fund has had to deal with, almost, bankrupt countries.

The Jupiter Saturn conjunction of 2000 falls in an Earth sign and we might expect that by the time of the conjunction itself, a return to the old ways of building a secure capital base before spending would be one result. The days of running up large credit bills on the expectation of secure earnings may well be over and a return to prudent saving, thrift and conservation is likely in the coming years.

From a currency point of view, it should be noted that a similar planetary combination, way back in the 1790s, saw the demise of the French assignat of the period. If history is to repeat, then the currency most under threat in 2000 will be the pound sterling.

However, it is not just a conjunction of Jupiter with Saturn that takes place in May 2000, but a square pattern to the planet Uranus then

in the sign of Aquarius. Uranus is the planet of the unexpected and also the planet associated with new technologies. We have been forewarned of the 'Millennium' computer bug and it may be that this will have its most serious knock-on effect by May of 2000. Looked at from a purely financial point of view, we might wonder whether or not there will be a collapse of the banking system worldwide; perhaps caused by difficulties with the computers involved in 'hole in the wall' banking. Another possibility is banking mayhem caused through the introduction of new currencies around this time. This does not augur well for the Euro, being proposed for several European countries.

It is not at all easy to say which Sun signs will have most difficulty with these changes. Given that the planet line-up takes place in the sign of Taurus, one of the Fixed signs of the zodiac. The term 'Fixed' is used to describe the signs of Taurus, Leo, Scorpio and Aquarius: one each of the Earth, Fire, Water and Air signs. The term 'Fixed' describes a steadfast, determined approach to life. It is also true that it brings qualities of stubbornness and forthrightness. Taureans generally take a practical approach and, forewarned of the pending May 2000 difficulty, will make some safeguards either through spreading their risk, which is unusual for them, or by stockpiling goods which may be in short supply. Those of another fixed sign, Scorpio, will have their fears confirmed as to the untrustworthiness of banks. Since Scorpios have always been aware of this possibility and since they experienced personal difficulties during the 1980s and early 1990s, they are fortunate in having experience on which to fall back. We may be assured that they will be able to cope and to protect their interests well. It is the Leos and Aquarians who are most likely to be shocked by what takes place and be most affected by it. It would be as well for those of these signs to discuss their business affairs with advisors and to make provision for awkward eventualities.

Those born under the signs of Taurus, Cancer, Leo, Virgo, Libra, Scorpio, Sagittarius and Capricorn are best placed to rebuild their capital reserves. Each of these signs understands the 'language' of saving and will be able to revert to natural traits without too much difficulty. Aries people may find the task hard since they will be

required to undo a whole behavioural pattern that has allowed them to have what they want as and when they wanted it. For slightly different reasons, the Geminis will experience difficulties. No amount of talking is going to be able to persuade those who have finance to lend it to them without the Gemini having sufficient collateral.

With Uranus, the planet of the unexpected and ruler of Aquarius, passing through that sign until 2002, those born under the sign of Aquarius will be having to cope with dramatic changes in their lives which, inevitably, will affect their finances. As we saw in the section about Aquarians, the desire to embrace new challenges is on a collision course with the Aquarian natural resistance to anything other than that which is tried and trusted. It is this sign, therefore, that will feel the pressure of the May 2000 build-up more than any other sign. Even Pisceans, who are adept at changing direction when necessary and whose ability to do so is sorely tested by the May 2000 line-up, will not feel the pressures as keenly as our Aquarian friends. For Aquarians, who are intellectually willing to embrace new challenges and yet are shocked emotionally by what is demanded of them, the speed at which events unfold will cause them to have to undertake dramatic changes in their own lives. The result of this will be the painful learning curve of realising that regular (an alien concept) payments toward a savings plan will secure their position.

Difficulties in May 2000 are caused by the extraordinary tension created by Jupiter and Saturn beginning their new cycle, whilst simultaneously Uranus, at 90 degrees from both, is at an important point in its relationship to each. In combination with the alignment of New and Full Moons in the course of the month, the world may expect extreme tension. The fact that this tension exists across Fixed signs of the zodiac suggests a degree of intransigence and consequent discomfort not seen since the First World War. By no means would one wish to predict war as being inevitable through this period; nevertheless, this will be a testing time for humanity.

Polarisation of the 'haves' and the 'have nots' could make for a difficult time socially. For us all, it will become more common to consider what it is that we truly need in terms of material benefits.

The accent toward spiritual riches will become more dominant in the years ahead. For those not already embarked on this path, the coming years will coincide with a steep learning curve as they evaluate their real priorities.

On a very practical level, it is likely that the banking community will experience difficulties with electronic transaction equipment in May 2000 so that lack of cash, on a very real basis, will confront many. Those who have the gift for bartering will be in a better position to weather the storm than others.

It is not easy to conclude this book with an upbeat forecast for the future. We live in interesting times. Change is inevitable. Those who are able to see the signals and adapt to the radically different conditions may gain the most material success. But material and financial success is not everything and there will be many who feel better off in a quite different sense through detaching themselves as best they are able and, instead, working compassionately and understandingly with others.

Finally, this book would not be complete without an exercise for all signs which might help prepare for the financial challenges of the coming decade. There are two periods to concentrate on. The first is to think how best to be ready for possible financial worldwide crisis after May 2000. This means spreading risk and ensuring that potential for staying financially afloat is not sabotaged by lack of preparedness. Being alert to dangers is one thing. Having contingencies plans is another. Each person from each sign will have to develop their skills to cope whilst ensuring that any weaknesses do not exacerbate problems. The worst case scenario is to assume that all capital and investments are temporarily wiped out. How would you start again?

The second exercise is linked to 2008. That year, Pluto will start to make its way into the next sign: Capricorn. It will stay in that sign until 2010. This promises to be an exciting time for the development of new small businesses built on the collapsed ruins of larger organisations. Visualise having a very large sum of money available to you in 2010. By this time, cracks in larger companies and corporations are likely to be obvious. Think about which bits of

companies you would like to be in a position to buy at knock down prices and how you would rebuild these.

Lastly, for money to be an enriching energy, it has to work to the benefit of many. Imagine yourself as a philanthropist in 2005. Any banking problems will be in the process of resolution and many changes will still be being made in the way in which currency is used. There will be many people across the world deeply damaged by what has taken place. Think of how you would like to assist them. Other than your cash and your philanthropy, is there a talent or skill that you could share? What legacy would like to leave? Next think of how you could start to make your way toward that goal.

5

MAY 2000

*I*t is exceedingly rare for an astrologer to isolate one period of time as warranting extra attention. Every moment, and therefore every chart or horoscope, fascinates an astrologer. However, within the astrological community there is a certain fascination with the pattern that the planets will make in the month of May 2000 (see p. 77).

It is during this month that the two planets, Jupiter and Saturn will form their next conjunction (i.e. as viewed from Earth they will appear to be in a straight line). This is something that they do every twenty years or so. The conjunction that takes place in 2020 will be in an Air sign and the two after that will also be in Air signs. The conjunctions then move through their Water and Fire phases before returning to Earth signs.

To recap, the Jupiter Saturn conjunctions of the twentieth century have all been in Earth signs except for the one in 1981 which took place in the sign of Libra. The 1981 Air conjunction saw the dawn of the 'yuppie' era. Between the time of the conjunction and the opposition just nine years later, prices rose dramatically. At the same time, countries and individuals were able to borrow more and more. Levels of debt and credit reached all time highs.

Soon after the opposition of 1989, it was realised that these levels could not be sustained. A correction would be inevitable. One possible outcome could be that there will be considerable emphasis placed on the need to save before purchase in the period up until the next opposition in 2010. After then, it is possible that there will be a return to a mini-yuppie period before the 2020 conjunction and an escalation of credit and debt in the ten years after that.

The May 2000 conjunction is special not just because it is the last of the Earth series for some time, but because it takes place at a time when Uranus will be reaching a point in its cycle when it will be 90 degrees from both Jupiter and Saturn.

Jupiter and Uranus come together (conjoin) every 12 or so years. En route, there are times when the two planets are 90 degrees, then 180 degrees and then 90 degrees from one another. In May 2000, Jupiter will have moved 90 degrees away from Uranus. Jupiter and Uranus were last in conjunction in 1997. Uranus is associated with new technology and exciting breakthroughs. Jupiter is associated with growth and expansion. It is recognised then that when the two planets come together, that these are likely to be times when something innovative grabs the headlines and when the world in general is excited at the prospect of a new advance.

When the two planets lie at 90 degrees – or are in a square – to one another, there are similar headlines, but we now hear about the problems that the new inventions are facing and perhaps causing. We read of the efforts made to redress problems and see scientists and technical people straining to resolve major difficulties.

In May 2000, not only does Uranus square Jupiter, it will also square Saturn. The Saturn–Uranus cycle describes the tussle between old and new, traditional and modern. It is at these times that we find authority struggling to cope with new innovations. We also find new ideas being challenged by those who would prefer to stay with the tried and familiar.

Although Neptune will be out of range of an exact 90 degree aspect, its closeness to Uranus suggests that Neptune will have some effect on these squares. This suggests that the problems will be confused and possibly indeterminate, and that they will affect far, far more people than might otherwise be the case. 'Boundaries' is not a word associated with Neptune. Neptunian effects tend therefore to be far reaching. We may consider then that any problems which do occur will have both wide-ranging implications and uncontrollable effect.

This does not auger well for financial matters. Those working within the banking community – and the Jupiter Saturn conjunction will occur in the very bank-orientated sign of Taurus, are likely to experience a very hard time indeed this month.

Uranus rules electronics and acts chaotically and unexpectedly. It is possible that its square to the Jupiter Saturn conjunction will coincide with a massive electronic failure which brings banking – if only temporarily – to a halt. Neptune's involvement would seem to indicate that this will have effect worldwide and that major fraud might be involved also.

Should there be an electronic failure this will have huge implications for the cash flow not just of individuals but companies. Some companies may not manage to survive this period. More importantly some banks may not be able to cope either with the problem itself or with the aftermath. It is highly likely that younger generations who have no experience of pen and paper accounting will find this period exceedingly difficult. It is also possible that older generations, whilst able to resort to old methods of working, will be swamped by the sheer quantity and complexity of trades involved.

On 3 May 2000, no fewer than six planets will all be in the sign of Taurus and in square to either Neptune or Uranus. The effect of their combined gravitational pull on the Earth may be such that more than one natural catastrophe occurs. Uranus's presence would indicate that we should all be on red alert for the unexpected. Insurance companies are already primed as to the potential risks of this period. Individuals would be wise to take note of the period and to be as prepared as they can to cope with the unexpected.

MAY 2000
Natal Chart
3 May 2000
06:20 BST – 1:00
London, UK
51N30 000W10
Geocentric
Tropical
0° Aries
True Node

00° ♑ 00'

00° ♒ 00'

00° ♐ 00'

♀ 12° ♐ 18' R

♆ 06° ♒ 34'

♅ 20° ♒ 37'

00° ♓ 00°

00° ♏ 00'

10

9

11

8

12

7

00° ♈ 00'

00° ♎ 00'

1

6

00° ♂ 16'
♌ 02° ♉ 35'
☽ 06° ♉ 12'
♀ 13° ♉ 05'
☿ 16° ♉ 42'
☉ 19° ♉ 28'
♃ 29° ♉ 35'
♄

2

5

00° ♉ 00'

00° ♍ 00'

3

4

00° ♊ 00'

00° ♋ 00'

00° ♌ 00'

fURTHER READING

Financial and business astrology is only now coming into vogue. As such, there is little published for the layperson. The organisations listed below will give details of specialist books and articles. This short reading list will assist those who want to take the information from this book a step further.

Astrology Really Works, written and published by The Magi Society.
Investing by the Stars, by Henry Weingarten published by McGraw-Hill.
Money and the Markets, by Graham Bates and Jane Bowles published by Aquarius.
Money: How to find it with astrology, by Lois Rodden published by Fowlers.

USEFUL ADDRESSES

CONSULTATIONS

The newly formed International Society of Business Astrologers
Karen Boesen, Frederikssundsvej 128 C, 2700 Bronshoj, Denmark

The author is a member of the Board of ISBA and can be contacted
at 138 Springbank Road, London SE13 6SU, United Kingdom

Astrologers may also be found through any of the organisations
listed below.

ARC NODES

The Urania Trust is a founding member of ARC, Astrological
Registration and Communication. ARC is an open, international
network which holds up to date information on schools, groups and
individual astrologers, and on what is going on in astrology in
different parts of the world. The following list of ARC nodes is not
comprehensive but any one of these will be able to direct you to
your local ARC node.

UNITED KINGDOM

Urania Trust, 396 Caledonian Road, London N1 1DN.
Tel: +44 (0)171 700 0639

Australia

Lynda Hill, 20 Harley Road, Avalon NSW 2107. Tel: 61 2 918 9539
Brian Clark, The Chiron Centre, 407 Johnston Street, Abbotsford,
Victoria 3067. Tel: +61 3 419 4566

Canada

Anne Black, Director, Astro*Linguistics Institute, 2182 Cubbon
Drive, Victoria, British Columbia V8R 1R5. Tel: +1 604 370 1874

Robin Armstrong, PO Box 5265, Station 'A', Toronto, Ontario
M5W 1N5. Tel: +1 416 368 0265

South Africa

Astrological Society of South Africa, PO Box 2968, Rivonia 2128.
Tel: +27 11 864 1436

United States

Mark Pottenger, Research Director, International Society for
Astrological Research inc (ISAR), PO Box 38613, Los Angeles,
CA 90038-8613. Tel: +1 805 525 0461

Organisations and schools

United Kingdom

The Faculty of Astrological Studies, BM 7470, London WC1N 3XX.
Tel: +44 (0)700 790143

The Mayo School of Astrology, Alvana Gardens, Tregavethan, Truro
TR4 9EN. Tel: +44 (0)1872 560048

The Company of Astrologers, PO Box 3001, London N1 1LY.
Tel: +44 (0)227 362427

Astrological Association of Great Britain, BM Box 3935, London
WC1N 3XX. Tel: +44 (0)171 700 3746

The Astrological Lodge of London, 50 Gloucester Place, London W1H 3HJ.

British Astrological and Psychic Society, c/o Robert Denholm House, Bletchingley Road, Nutfield, Redhill, Surrey RH1 4HW.

The English Huber School, PO Box 118, Knutsford, Cheshire WA16 8TG. Tel: +44 (0)1565 651131

The Centre for Psychological Astrology, BM Box 1815, London WC1N 3XX. Tel: +44 (0)181 749 2330

Australia

Federation of Australian Astrologers
c/o Lynda Hill, 20 Harley Road, Avalon, NSW 2107.

Canada

Canadian Association for Astrological Association
Murray Souva, 4191 Stonemason Crescent, Mississauga, Ontario L5L 2Z6.

Toronto Chapter of N.C.G.R
c/o The Star Centre, PO Box 5265, Station "A", Toronto, Ontario.

Association Canadiennes des Astrologues Francophones (ACAF)
CP 1715, Succ "B", Montreal (Quebec) H3B 3L3.

South Africa

The Southern Cross Academy of Astrology
Anita Noyes-Smith, P.O. Box 781147, Sandton, SA 2146.

United States of America

National Council for Geocosmic Research (NCGR)
Margaret Meister, PO Box 501078, Malabar, FL 32950.

Association for Astrological Networking (AFAN)
8306 Wilshere Blvd, Suite 537, Beverley Hills, CA 90211.

Kepler College of Astrological Arts and Sciences
4518 University Way NE, Suite 213 Seattle, WA 98105.

American Federation of Astrologers
c/o Robert Cooper, PO Box 22040, Tempe, AZ 85285-2040.

WEBSITES

What follows is a list of interesting sites available as of January 1998

www.users.globalnet.co.uk/~urania/index.htm
www.astrocollege.com
www.astrologer.com
www.astrologer.com.aanet
www.astrology-world.com
www.astrology.org.uk
www.electric-ephemeris.com
www.astrology.co.uk
www.equinox.uk.com
www.stars.org/isar/
www.astrology.net
www.afund.com (financial astrology website)

Other titles in this series

Astral Projection   Is it possible for the soul to leave the body at will? In this book the traditional techniques used to achieve astral projection are described in a simple, practical way, and Out of the Body and Near Death Experiences are also explored.

Astrology   An exploration of how astrology helps us to understand ourselves and other people. Learn how to draw up and interpret a horoscope.

Astrology and Health   This book explains simply the symbolic richness of the zodiac signs and how they can illuminate our experience of health.

Becoming Prosperous   A guide to how *anyone* can feel and become more prosperous by focusing on state of mind and conscious thought. Practical exercises help readers develop personal strategies to become more prosperous, both financially and emotionally.

Chakras   The body's energy centres, the chakras, can act as gateways to healing and increased self-knowledge. This book shows you how to work with chakras in safety and with confidence.

Channelling   Channelling is the process by which ancient knowledge and wisdom are tapped and reclaimed for the enlightenment and enrichment of life in the present. This book offers simple techniques to become channels of awareness.

Chinese Horoscopes   In the Chinese system of horoscopes, the year of birth is all-important. *Chinese Horoscopes for beginners* tells you how to determine your own Chinese horoscope, what personality traits you are likely to have, and how your fortunes may fluctuate in years to come.

Dowsing   People all over the world have used dowsing since the earliest times. This book shows how to start dowsing – what to use, what to dowse, and what to expect when subtle energies are detected.

Dream Interpretation   This fascinating introduction to the art and science of dream interpretation explains how to unravel the meaning behind dream images to interpret your own and other people's dreams.

Earth Mysteries   What can we learn from observing the earth and the remains of our prehistoric ancestors? Explore ley lines, earth energies, astro-archaeology and sacred landscapes to expand your consciousness and achieve a better perspective on existence.

Enlightenment   Learn how you can experience primary enlightenment through tried-and-tested exercises which offer the tools to help you to find your own unique truth.

Feng Shui   This beginner's guide to the ancient art of luck management will show you how to increase your good fortune and well-being by harmonising your environment with the natural energies of the earth.

Freeing Your Intuition   Develop awareness of your intuition and make your own good fortune, increase your creative output and learn to recognise what you *know*, not just what you think.

Gems and Crystals   For centuries gems and crystals have been used as an aid to healing and meditation. This guide tells you all you need to know about choosing, keeping and using stones to increase your personal awareness and improve your well-being.

The Goddess   This book traces the development, demise and rebirth of the Goddess, looking at the worship of Her and retelling myths from all over the world.

Graphology   Graphology, the science of interpreting handwriting to reveal personality, is now widely accepted and used throughout the world. This introduction will enable you to make a comprehensive analysis of your own and other people's handwriting to reveal the hidden self.

The Healing Powers of Plants   Plants and herbs can be used to enhance everyday life through aromatherapy, herbalism, homoeopathy and colour therapy. Their power can be used in cosmetics, meditation and home decoration.

Herbs for Magic and Ritual   This book looks at the well-known herbs and the stories attached to them. There is information on the use of herbs in essential oils and incense, and on their healing and magical qualities.

I Ching   The roots of *I Ching* or the *Book of Changes* lie in the time of the feudal mandarin lords of China, but its traditional wisdom is still relevant today. Using the original poetry in its translated form, this introduction traces its history, survival and modern-day applications.

Interpreting Signs and Symbols   The history of signs and symbols is traced in this book from their roots to the modern age. It also examines the way psychiatry uses symbolism, and the significance of doodles.

The Language of Flowers   Flowers can and do heal us, both emotionally and physically, with their smell and their beauty. By looking at these areas, together with superstitions associated with flowers and their links with New Age subjects, the author gives advice on how to enhance your life with flowers.

Love Signs   This is a practical introduction to the astrology of romantic relationships. It explains the different roles played by each of the planets, focusing particularly on the position of the Moon at the time of birth.

The Magic and Mystery of Trees   This book explores the many meanings of trees, from myth and folklore through ritual and seasonal uses to their 'spiritual essence' and esoteric meanings.

Meditation   This beginner's guide gives simple, clear instructions to enable you to start meditating and benefiting from this ancient mental discipline immediately. The text is illustrated throughout by full-colour photographs and line drawings.

Mediumship   Whether you want to become a medium yourself, or simply understand what mediumship is about, this book will give you the grounding to undertake a journey of discovery into the spirit realms.

The Moon and You   The phase of the Moon when you were born radically affects your personality. This book looks at nine lunar types – how they live, love, work and play, and provides simple tables to find out the phase of your birth.

The Norse Tradition   This book gives a comprehensive introduction to the Norse Tradition, a vibrant, living current within the multitude of spiritual paths of Paganism.

Numerology   Despite being scientifically based, numerology requires no great mathematical talents to understand. This introduction gives you all the information you will need to understand the significance of numbers in your everyday life.

Numerology and Relationships   This guide takes you step by step through the hidden meanings behind the important numbers in your life to discover more about you, your compatibilities with others and the crucial relationships with your parents, partner and children.

Pagan Gods   Looking at ancient gods and old stories, this guide explores the social and psychological issues affecting the role of men today. In these pages men of all ages and persuasions can find inspiration.

Paganism   Pagans are true Nature worshippers who celebrate the cycles of life. This guide describes pagan festivals and rituals and takes a detailed look at the many forms of paganism practised today.

Palmistry   Palmistry is the oldest form of character reading still in use. This illustrated guide shows you exactly what to look for and how to interpret what you find.

Qabalah   The Qabalah is an ancient Jewish system of spiritual knowledge centred on the Tree of Life. This guide explains how it can be used in meditation and visualisation, and links it to the chakras, yoga, colour therapy, crystals, Tarot and numerology.

Reiki   In this book you will find advice on how to learn Reiki, its application and potential, and you will be shown an avenue of understanding of this simple, practical technique which offers pain relief through meditation and laying-on of hands.

Reincarnation and You   What happens to us after death? Here, you will find practical advice on using dreams, recurrent visions, déjà vu and precognition to access hidden parts of your consciousness which recall or anticipate past and future lives.

Runes   The power of the runes in healing and giving advice about relationships and life in general has been acknowledged since the time of the Vikings. This book shows how runes can be used in our technological age to increase personal awareness and stimulate individual growth.

Shamanism   Shamanic technique offers direct contact with Spirit, vivid self-knowledge and true kinship with plants, animals and the planet Earth. This book describes the shamanic way, the wisdom of the Medicine Wheel and power animals.

Some Traditional African Beliefs   Fortune telling and healing are two of the aspects of traditional African spiritual life looked at in this book. Exercises based on ancient beliefs show you how to use the environment to find ways to harmonise modern urban life in a practical way.

Spiritual Healing   All healing starts with self, and the Universal Power which makes this possible is available to everyone. In this book there are exercises, techniques and guidelines to follow which will enable you to heal yourself and others spiritually.

Star Signs   This detailed analysis looks at each of the star signs in turn and reveals how your star sign affects everything about you. This book shows you how to use this knowledge in your relationships and in everyday life.

Tantric Sexuality   Tantric Buddhists use sex as a pleasurable path to enlightenment. This guide offers a radically different and exciting new dimension to sex, explaining practical techniques in a clear and simple way.

Tarot   Tarot cards have been used for many centuries. This guide gives advice on which sort to buy, where to get them and how to use them. The emphasis is on using the cards positively, as a tool for gaining self-knowledge, while exploring present and future possibilities.

Visualisation   This introduction to visualisation, a form of self-hypnosis widely used by Buddhists, will show you how to practise the basic techniques – to relieve stress, improve your health and increase your sense of personal well-being.

Witchcraft   This guide to the ancient religion based on Nature worship answers many of the questions and uncovers the myths and misconceptions surrounding witchcraft. Mystical rituals and magic are explained and there is advice for the beginner on how to celebrate the Sabbats.

Working With Colour   Colour is the medicine of the future. This book explores the energy of each colour and its significance, gives advice on how colour can enhance our well-being, and gives ideas on using colour in the home and garden.

Your Psychic Powers   Are you psychic? This book will help you find out by encouraging you to look more deeply within yourself. Psychic phenomena such as precognitive dreams, out of body travels and visits from the dead are also discussed in this ideal stepping stone towards a more aware you.

To order this series

All books in this series are available from bookshops or, in case of difficulty, can be ordered direct from the publisher. Prices and availability subject to change without notice. Send your order with your name and address to: Hodder & Stoughton, Cash Sales Department, Bookpoint, 39 Milton Park, Abingdon, OXON, OX14 4TD, UK. If you have a credit card you may order by telephone – 01235 831700.

For sales in the following countries please contact:
UNITED STATES: Trafalgar Square (Vermont), Tel: 800 423 4525 (toll-free)
CANADA: General Publishing (Ontario), Tel: 445 3333
AUSTRALIA: Hodder & Stoughton (Sydney), Tel: 02 638 5299